WORKING AND PRESERVED
INDUSTRIAL
LOCOMOTIVES
FROM THE BILL REED COLLECTION

PETER TUFFREY

FONTHILL MEDIA

Nottinghamshire, Gedling Colliery

Andrew Barclay supplied 0-6-0ST, *Catherine*, works no. 1000, new to Gedling Colliery, Nottinghamshire, in 1903, and the locomotive stayed there throughout its working life. The photograph was taken during August 1967.

Fonthill Media Limited
www.fonthillmedia.com
office@fonthillmedia.com

This edition published in the United Kingdom 2012

British Library Cataloguing in Publication Data.
A catalogue record for this book is available from the British Library.

ISBN 978-1-78155-057-1 (PRINT)
ISBN 978-1-78155-147-9 (E-BOOK)

Typeset in 10 pt Sabon
Printed and bound in England.

Connect with us
facebook.com/fonthillmedia twitter.com/fonthillmedia

Contents

Leicestershire, Castle Donnington Power Station
RS&H 0-6-0ST *Castle Donnington Power Station no. 2* was photographed in June 1974. Both CDPS locomotives featured 16-in.-diameter cylinders, extended coal space ahead of the cab and a re-railing beam across the frame to prevent the locomotive falling completely between the rails in the event of a derailment.

Yorkshire, Newmarket Colliery
0-6-0ST locomotive, *Jess*, built by the Hunslet Engine Company in 1943, works no. 2876, is pictured at Newmarket Colliery, Yorkshire, on 16 September 1971. Just over two years later, the engine was scrapped on site by W. H. Arnott, Young & Co. Ltd of Bradford.

Acknowledgements

I am grateful for the assistance received from the following people: Catherine at Book Law Nottingham, Bob Darvil, Stuart Geeson, Bill Hudson, John Law, Hugh Parkin, Bill Reed, Alan Sutton (for his boundless energy and support once again).

A special thanks to my son Tristram for his general encouragement and help behind the scenes.

I have taken reasonable steps to verify the accuracy of the information in this book but it may contain errors or omissions. Any information that may be of assistance to rectify any problems will be gratefully received. Please contact me in writing: Peter Tuffrey, 8 Wrightson Avenue, Warmsworth, Doncaster, South Yorkshire, DN4 9QL.

Derbyshire, Wirksworth
Holwell no. 3, built by Black, Hawthorne & Co. Ltd in 1873, moved to Wirksworth from Harlaxton Ironstone Quarries, Derbyshire, during August 1946. Photographed in June 1970, *Holwell no. 3* moved to the Tanfield Railway Co., Marley Hill, Co. Durham, on 19 November 1977 where it is known as *Wellington*.

References

Ashforth, Philip J., Ian Bendall and Ken Plant, *Industrial Railways and Locomotives of Lincolnshire and Rutland*, 2010

Bendall, Ian R., *Industrial Locomotives of Nottinghamshire*, 1999

Bradley, V. J., *Industrial Locomotives of Yorkshire Part A: The National Coal Board including Opencast Disposal Points and British Coal in West and North Yorkshire*, 2002

Etherington, A. R. and I. R. Bendall, *Industrial Railways and Locomotives of Leicestershire and South Derbyshire*, 2006

Heaveyside, Tom, *Yorkshire's Last Days of Colliery Steam*, 2005

Hill, Geoffrey, *Industrial locomotives of Mid and South Glamorgan*, 2007

Industrial Railway Society, *Industrial Railways and Locomotives of South Yorkshire: The Coal Industry – 1947-1964*, 2007

Industrial Railway Society, *Industrial Locomotives Including Preserved and Minor Railway Locomotives*, 2012

Old Glory Vintage Restoration Today No. 27 May 1992

Railway Bylines, *Prince of Wales Colliery*, by Adrian Booth, September 1999

Railway Bylines, *Ackton Hall Colliery: Tales From the Fitting Shop*, January 2000

Railway Bylines, *Through the Streets*, January 2000

Railway Bylines, *Uppingham at Middlepeak*, September 2001

Railway Bylines, *Seaham Harbour and its Railways*, September 2002

Railway Bylines, Volume 10 Issue 4, March 2005

Railway Bylines, Volume 12 Issue 1, December 2006

Railway Bylines, Volume 14 Issue 2, January 2009

Shill, R. M., *Industrial Locomotives of South Staffordshire*, 1993

Smith, Andrew and Roy Etherington, Eds., *Industrial Railway Society Preliminary Draft Industrial Railways and Locomotives of West Yorkshire*, 2004

Waywell, Robin, *Industrial Locomotives of Buckinghamshire Bedfordshire and Northamptonshire*, 2001

Introduction

Photography has been Bill Reed's life-long passion. He's now 78 and still carries a camera (a cine one these days) around with him nearly everywhere he goes. The subject has always been railways – at home, in Europe, Eastern Europe and America.

Born in Nottingham, Bill started work at the city's Victoria Station and his interest in railways grew. He was helped along by enthusiast Freddie Guildford who encouraged him to take pictures and taught him the rudiments of developing and printing. Switching jobs, Bill became an engine cleaner and embarked on the long road to realising his ambition of one day becoming a driver, but this was cut short when National Service intervened. Always looking for an opportunity to exercise his love of photography and railways, Bill joined the RAF's Photographic club (for a month) and whilst abroad he used recently acquired cameras: a Kodak Box Brownie and an Agfa Isolette III to take pictures at the Shed in Singapore and many more locations.

Once demobbed, Bill acquired an Agfa Super Isolette, and in subsequent years used this to take many of his pictures. In time he worked as a fireman on steam locomotives and then became a driver on diesel electrics. In the 1950s and 1960s he took many black & white pictures and colour slides of steam engines working mainlines, branch lines, resting in motive power depots and undergoing repairs on works. A selection of the pictures he took around Nottingham formed the basis of an earlier book *The Last Days of Steam in Nottinghamshire*, published by Alan Sutton in 2010.

Bill admits that he, like many other railway photographers, concentrated on capturing steam locomotives in industrial areas once they began to disappear elsewhere. He visited local collieries in Nottinghamshire, Derbyshire, Staffordshire and Yorkshire, as well as the iron ore workings in other parts of the country. He even travelled further afield to Wales and Scotland to photograph industrial locos working in their final days. Looking at Bill's pictures from this period it is quickly realised that access was unrestricted. Nobody questioned or was suspicious of what he was doing. It was a fantastic time for railway photographers.

It is tempting to suggest that in the late 1960s people began to wake up to the fact that very few steam locomotives (main line or even from the smaller classes) had been preserved. So, there began a quest to save large numbers of industrial engines in both standard and narrow gauges.

In time, preservation lines and heritage centres began to appear and it was only natural that Bill would visit them and take pictures. Examples may be seen at Carnforth, Knebworth and Lytham. Sadly these three, along with a few others, are no longer in existence, but thankfully their stock may be seen working elsewhere.

It is interesting to observe that some locomotives Bill photographed as 'working', may also be seen in preservation. So arguably, this collection of pictures, for the most part, illustrates industrial steam in its last days and in the first years of preservation.

Some 1,200 black & white negatives and colour slides were scanned to make the required selection of approximately 225 pictures. The task was by no means easy because Bill has visited so many different and interesting locations.

My research has been assisted by enlisting the help of several members of the Industrial Railway Society, in particular their Records Officer Bob Darvil. The society's books have been analysed meticulously as they are marvellous, painstaking pieces of research.

Bill's photographs make us thankful that we have preserved a number of industrial steam locomotives. Long may they survive on preserved lines and heritage centres throughout the UK, Europe and the rest of the world.

Chapter 1
Aberdeenshire to Derbyshire

Aberdeenshire, Aberdeen Gas Works

The Aberdeen Gas Works site saw major reconstruction work in 1919. The locomotive stock was also increased with the purchase of a saddle tank 0-4-0 from Andrew Barclay Sons & Co. of Kilmarnock. It took the name of one of the Works' earlier locomotives, Aberdeen Corporation Gas Works no. 3 – later renamed Aberdeen Gas Works no. 3. The engine was fitted with covers over the wheels and motion for safety reasons. Steam-hauled railway traffic ceased on the gas works site in 1964. In time, no. 3 went for preservation at Ferryhill, but it is presently at the Grampian Transport Museum, Alford. The locomotive is seen here in its post-1948 livery, but it is currently displayed at Alford in an earlier green livery.

Opposite above: Bedfordshire, Whipsnade
The Great Whipsnade Railway, originally called the Whipsnade & Umfolozi Railway, was built by Bill McAlpine in 1970 with the line opening on 26 August of that year. It is a 2-ft-6-in.-(762-mm) narrow-gauge line and forms a two-mile-long loop, taking it through several animal paddocks. *Excelsior*, a *Brazil* class, Type 0-4-2ST was built by Kerr Stuart & Co., works no. 1049, and was constructed at the former California Works in Stoke on Trent in August 1908. The photograph was taken in July 1976. A new boiler was fitted to the locomotive in 2008.

Opposite below: Buckinghamshire, Quainton Road
'Austerity' 0-6-0ST locomotive no. 3850 *Juno* was built by Hunslet in 1958 for Stewarts & Lloyds, Rutland. Having outlived its usefulness in 1968, *Juno* was acquired by the Ivatt Trust and moved to the Buckinghamshire Railway Centre where it is seen here in April 1973. In May 2009, *Juno* was moved to the Isle of Wight to join the Ivatt Trust's other locomotives. In October 2010 the loco was placed on loan to the National Railway Museum. The museum's website states: 'There were 484 locomotives built to this design, and around 70 still survive. However, *Juno* is the last untouched and original example, having only worked for 11 years before retirement.'

Above: Buckinghamshire, Quainton Road
Over a period of about fifty years from 1882, the Hunslet Engine Company of Leeds constructed many narrow-gauge locomotives for Welsh slate quarries. 0-4-0ST, no. 779, built in 1902, was a typical example. It was supplied new to the Asheton-Smith family who owned Dinorwic Slate Quarry, Llanberis, North Wales, and was named no. 3. Five years later it adopted the name *Holy War* after one of the owner's winning race horses. The engine remained in service until 1967, becoming the last steam loco to work in a British slate quarry. In 1968 it was taken to the Buckinghamshire Railway Centre at Quainton, and is seen there in this picture taken in April 1973. It is currently owned by the Bala Lake Railway at Llanuwchllyn, Gwynedd, and has been there since December 1975.

Cambridge, Richard Duce's scrap yard

Both photographs on this page were taken by Bill Reed from a moving train whilst he was travelling from Nottingham to Cambridge. The top picture shows an unidentified Kitson 0-6-0ST locomotive; the one below an unidentified Peckett 0-4-0ST. The view is in Richard Duce's scrap yard.

Buckinghamshire, Quainton Road

Hunslet 0-6-0ST, works no. 1690, *Cunarder*, no. 47160, was built in 1931 – one of six locos supplied for use on the construction of the King George V dock at Southampton. Thereafter the locomotive worked for a variety of firms until it was purchased for preservation by Messrs G. S. Simms, D. Britton and G. Kingham and moved to Quainton in April 1969. Whilst in commercial use *Cunarder* was retubed twice and had a new firebox fitted. A further set of tubes was installed whilst the loco was at Quainton, leaving there in March 1976. The locomotive is currently with the South Coast Steam Co. Ltd, Portland, Dorset.

Cornwall, Bodmin & Wenford Railway

0-4-0ST *Alfred*, works no. 3058, was erected in 1953 by Stafford locomotive manufacturer W. G. Bagnall for use at Par Harbour in Cornwall. *Alfred* was named after the harbour manager Alfred Truscott. The locomotive arrived at Par in 1954 and was kept in service until 1977. A year later, *Alfred* was moved to the Cornish Steam Locomotive Preservation Society site at Bugle where a vacuum brake was fitted so that it could haul passenger trains. In 1987 the CSLPS had to move, and so the locomotive found a new home on the Bodmin & Wenford Railway.

Denbighshire, Llangollen

Built by Kitsons of Leeds in 1932, this 0-6-0ST locomotive, works no. 5459, was delivered to the Longbridge Austin Motor Company Works where it was known as *Austin no. 1*. In November 1975 the loco was purchased on behalf of the Flint & Deeside Railway Society by Burtonwood Brewery. It was stored at Prestatyn until the society moved to Llangollen in 1975. *No. 1* was photographed at Llangollen Station in April 1977. For a time the loco was known as *Burtonwood Brewer*, but later reverted to its original name *Austin no. 1*. A rebuild occurred in 2000 and since that time it has been available for hire.

Derbyshire, Bailey Brook Colliery

The last of the deep-mine pits to be opened in the Heanor area was Ormonde Colliery. It was sunk by the Butterley Company in 1906, and production began in 1908. This led to the closure of the neighbouring Bailey Brook Colliery in 1938. But the Bailey Brook loco shed remained in use for servicing the locos which shunted at Ormonde Colliery until 1966 when it was moved to the latter location. 0-6-0ST, *Butterley no. 32* was built by W. Bagnall in 1940, works no. 2621, and delivered new to the Butterley Co. at Ripley Colliery, Derbyshire, in March 1940. Sometime before 'Vesting Day' (1 January 1947), according to the *IRR No. 77*, June 1978, 'she had migrated to the nearby Bailey Brook colliery.' The engine was photographed on 18 June 1955 and scrapped at Bailey Brook by 1963.

Derbyshire, Bailey Brook
W. Bagnall built 0-6-0ST *Butterley no. 30*, works no. 2604, in 1939.

Derbyshire, Bailey Brook
0-6-0ST, works no. 2056, B.C. 29 was built by Peckett in 1944. The engine was delivered new to the Butterley Co. at Bailey Brook and scrapped on site there by William Bush, Alfreton, in December 1963.

Derbyshire Brookhill Colliery, Pinxton
Brookhill Colliery was an extension to the Pinxton Colliery Company's pits, and sinking began in February 1908. The first 1,000 tons of coal were turned on 3 November 1910 and the colliery was connected to the rail network via a GNR colliery line. The colliery closed in 1969. Andrew Barclay built 0-4-0ST, works no. 905, in 1901. The locomotive was ex-James Oakes & Company before moving to Pye Hill Colliery, then to Cotes Park Colliery, Derbyshire, and latterly to Brookhill in 1949. Photographed on 25 June 1962, the engine was scrapped on site by May 1966. To the rear is 0-6-0DM *Emfour 9*, works no. D1114, built by Hudswell Clarke in 1958. The locomotive was supplied new to Brookhill and moved to Bentinck Colliery by March 1969.

Opposite above: Derbyshire Brookhill Colliery, Pinxton
Robert Stephenson & Co., Newcastle-on-Tyne, built 0-6-0ST, works no. 4156, in 1937. The engine was delivered new to Appleby-Frodingham Steel Co. Ltd, Scunthorpe, Lincolnshire, and was rebuilt there during the 1950s. After spells at Bestwood Central Workshops and Linby Colliery, the locomotive moved to Brookhill in August 1967, which coincides with the date the photograph was taken. It was scrapped on site in May 1969.

Opposite below: Derbyshire Brookhill Colliery, Pinxton
Emfour 2 0-6-0T is seen at Brookhill in August 1967. The engine was built by Hudswell Clarke in 1954, works no. 1877, and was supplied new to the colliery. The engine was scrapped on site by Thos W. Ward Ltd in May 1969.

Derbyshire Brookhill Colliery, Pinxton
This photograph shows the 0-6-0ST which was formerly named *Cotes Park No. 2*. The locomotive
had moved to Brookhill from Cotes Park Colliery by May 1963. Built by Hunslet in 1944, works
no. 3197, the locomotive was ex-WD France by May 1947, and stored for a time at Moor Green
Colliery. Photographed during August 1967, by April 1968 the engine had been scrapped.

Derbyshire Brookhill Colliery, Pinxton
0-6-0ST, works no. 1924, was delivered new to Annesley Colliery by Peckett's in 1937, but returned
to the builders for repairs between (possibly) May 1954 and July 1955. The engine was ex-A
Winning Colliery, before moving to Bentinck Colliery in November 1962. A move to Brookhill
occurred in January 1967, and the photograph was taken in August of that year. By April 1968, the
loco had been scrapped.

Derbyshire Brookhill Colliery, Pinxton

0-6-0T, *Emfour no. 2*, built by Hudswell Clarke in 1954, works no. 1877, is pictured alongside 0-6-0T *Emfour no. 4*. The latter engine was built by Hudswell Clarke, works no. 1879, in 1954, and delivered new to the colliery. *Emfour no. 4* moved to Kirkby colliery by May 1960.

Derbyshire Brookhill Colliery, Pinxton

Barclay's 0-4-0ST, *Benton* was supplied new to West Stanley Colliery, Co. Durham, in 1904, works no. 973. Later the loco moved to Burdale Quarries Ltd where it presumably acquired the name *Burdale*. In the *Industrial Locomotives of Nottinghamshire* (1999) it is stated that the locomotive was brought to Pinxton 'to be included in an auction and was never used here.'

Opposite above: Derbyshire Brookhill Colliery, Pinxton
Another view of 0-6-0T, *Emfour 4*, built by Hudswell Clarke, works no. 1879, in 1954. Both *Emfour 2* and *Emfour 4* were supplied new to Pinxton. After a move to Kirkby Colliery in May 1960, *Emfour 4* was scrapped in April 1967.

Opposite below: Derbyshire Brookhill Colliery, Pinxton
0-4-0ST *Peckett no. 2* was delivered new to Pinxton Collieries Ltd in 1939, works no. 1975. *The Industrial Railways of Nottinghamshire* (1999) notes that the locomotive was derelict by September 1957 and scrapped by May 1966.

Above: Derbyshire Brookhill Colliery, Pinxton
0-4-0WT, *Raven*, was delivered new to Sutton Colliery in 1913. The engine was built by H. W. Johnson & Co., works no. 56, and in subsequent years worked at Cotes Park Colliery and Pye Hill Colliery. It was scrapped at Brookhill by Wm Bush, Alfreton, by March 1950.

Derbyshire, Butterley
The Midland Railway, Butterley, near Ripley in Derbyshire, is a heritage railway and is operated by the Midland Railway Trust. 0-4-0 crane tank locomotive, *Stanton 24*, works no. 1875, dates from 1925. It is the sole survivor of seven similar engines built by Andrew Barclay for the Stanton & Staveley Company. Working at the Stanton Iron Works, Ilkeston, until 1967, and then the Riddings Iron Foundry for two years, *Stanton 24* was acquired by the Midland Railway in August 1971. The engine was successfully steamed in April 1973 and put to work at the Centre, but has since been retired. It can be seen on display in the Matthew Kirtley Exhibition Hall. The photograph was taken in August 1975.

Derbyshire, Cadley Hill Colliery, Castle Gresley

Cadley Hill Colliery, situated some 4 miles south of Burton-on-Trent, near Castle Gresley, opened in 1861. The colliery sidings were connected via a branch to the Midland Railway. Under NCB control the colliery became part of the East Midlands no. 7 Area. Rail traffic ceased in 1986 and the colliery closed in March 1988. Thereafter open-cast coal mining took place on the site and it was redeveloped. Bill Reed recalls that in the 1970s, the collieries were switching to diesel locomotives for their shunting, but the manager at Cadley Hill was a steam enthusiast and gathered cast offs from other collieries, overhauled some of them, and used steam 100 per cent for the railway system. Sentinel 0-6-0DH, works no. 10055, was built in 1961. The engine was ex-demo at WD Bicester and also had spells at Bath Yard loco shed, Leicestershire, and Measham Colliery, Leicestershire, before its arrival at Cadley Hill in February 1962. A further move to Baddesley Colliery, Warwickshire, occurred on 4 April 1983 (for spares). The photograph was taken on 17 May 1971.

Derbyshire, Cadley Hill Colliery, Castle Gresley

Florence no. 2 was ex-Florence Colliery and arrived at Cadley Hill during January 1975. The engine was built by W. Bagnall in 1953, works no. 3059. A Giesl ejector, with its characteristic rectangular tapered chimney, was fitted in April 1962. The *IRR No. 77*, June 1978, notes that in the spring of 1977 the locomotive was laid up for a rather unusual reason: 'a blackbird nested in the left hand motion and was allowed to rear her offspring in peace.' The NCB loaned the locomotive to the 'Battlefield Line Railway' when it was in need of further motive power for its passenger trains, and it arrived there for preservation on 12 May 1978. Ownership eventually passed to the Battlefield Railway, but without the resources for restoration, *Florence no.2* remained on static display at Shackerstone Station. Later a Foxfield Railway member bought the loco, and since its arrival in Staffordshire during 2000 it has undergone extensive restoration. The top picture was taken outside the shed at Cadley Hill on 7 July 1976, and the one below in August 1975.

Derbyshire, Cadley Hill Colliery, Castle Gresley
Built by Hunslet in 1943, works no. 2857, was ex-WD, having been used in France during the Second World War. The 'Austerity' 0-6-0ST returned to Leeds for a major overhaul from 1965-67, where it was fitted with an underfeed stoker. The engine worked at Dodworth Colliery until a transfer to Cadley Hill in January 1976. It was photographed on 7 July 1976 and named *Swiftsure* in 1979. The name was chosen by the then colliery manager. The locomotive is pictured in the shed situated at the east end of the screens. Built of red brick and corrugated sheet and fitted with side-moving 'concertina' doors, the shed could accommodate four locomotives on its two roads (one through road and one dead end). In February 1987, *Swiftsure* was taken into preservation at the Bodmin & Wenford Railway, Cornwall, but is currently located at the Strathspey Railway Co. Ltd.

Left: Derbyshire, Cadley Hill Colliery, Castle Gresley 0-6-0ST *Progress (Christoper until 1966)* was delivered new to Moira Colliery Co. Ltd in 1946, works no. 7298. It was built at Robert Stephenson & Hawthorns Ltd, Newcastle-upon-Tyne. Subsequently, the engine spent time at Bath Yard loco shed, Church Gresley Colliery and Measham Colliery, before moving to Cadley Hill during November 1967. The photograph was taken at the east end of the colliery sidings on 17 May 1971. The locomotive went into preservation from May 1988, and is currently at the Tanfield Railway, Tyneside Locomotive Museum Trust, Gateshead.

Opposite below: Derbyshire, Cadley Hill Colliery, Castle Gresley
No. 65, 0-6-0ST, was delivered new to Manvers Coal & Preparation Plant, South Yorkshire, in 1964, works no. 3889. Built by Hunslet, the engine moved to Cadley Hill in June 1965. Photographed in August 1975, no. 65 left Cadley Hill for Quainton Road Railway Society, Bucks., in January 1983.

Above and below: Derbyshire, Cadley Hill Colliery, Castle Gresley
0-6-0ST, *Cadley Hill no. 1*, was built by Hunslet in 1962, works no. 3851. The engine was ex-Nailstone CPP, arriving at Cadley Hill during November 1970. Featuring an underfeed stoker, it was the third from the last 'Austerity' loco ever to be built. It eventually took the nameplates of another loco carrying *Cadley Hill no. 1*; a Barclay/Hunslet rebuild which was scrapped in December 1970. The 1962 loco, painted green with red coupling rods, hand rails and buffer beams, was transferred to Snibston Colliery in March 1985. The top picture was taken on 29 May 1974 and the one below in June 1974. In both pictures the locomotive is seen near the loco shed.

Above and below: Derbyshire, Cadley Hill Colliery, Castle Gresley
Until 1970 this 0-6-0ST, built by W. Bagnall in 1954, works no. 3061, was NCB no. 6. Thereafter, it became *Empress*. The engine was delivered new to Bath Yard loco shed, arriving ex-Measham Colliery to Cadley Hill during July 1970. In April 1987 the engine went to R. Moore & H. Lewis c/o C.E.G.B. Rye House Power Station Hertfordshire. It is now preserved at Mangapps Railway Museum. The top picture shows the loco as no. 6, the one below as *Empress*.

Derbyshire, Dinting

The *Sunderland Echo* of 20 February 2008 notes that Doxford's Pallion ship yard in Sunderland operated a fleet of 0-4-0 steam locomotives, which were mostly crane tank engines. They were usually named after local districts and *Southwick*, seen here, was one of them. Built by Darlington-based Robert Stephenson & Hawthorns in 1942, works no. 7069, *Southwick*, along with four other crane tanks, was sold for preservation soon after railway working at Doxfords ended in February 1971. *Southwick* was photographed at Dinting in the 1970s but it has since relocated to the Keighley & Worth Valley Railway. ·

Derbyshire, Dinting

No. 680 was built by Baguely Cars Ltd (under the McEwan & Pratt name) in 1916. It was a 55/60-hp petrol paraffin locomotive. In the Edwardian era, petrol engines were beginning to be used on small railway locomotives as they were especially useful on small industrial sites where a steam locomotive could be uneconomical. The locomotive spent much of its working life, after some modifications, at the Aintree (Liverpool) Biscuit Factory of W. & R. Jacob & Co. Ltd. When the company closed its internal rail system in 1967, the loco was given to Beamish in 1968, but was on display at Dinting, where it is seen here, until 1990.

Derbyshire, Stanton Iron Works, Ilkeston

Stanton Ironworks' origins go back to 1846 when a Chesterfield man, Benjamin Smith, and his son Josiah, brought three blast-furnaces into production alongside the banks of the Nutbrook Canal. Their operation was served by Midland Railway, and Great Northern Railway connections opened during the latter half of the nineteenth century. Between 1865 and 1867, the Smith's operation grew, but they soon experienced financial difficulties and before long the business was taken over by the Crompton family. They owned the company for over eighty years, and by the early twentieth century, the business was named the Stanton Ironworks Company Ltd. This latter company was eventually taken over by Stewarts & Lloyds Ltd and merged with the Staveley Iron and Chemical Company Ltd in 1960 to form Stanton & Staveley. In 1967, Stewarts & Lloyds became part of the nationalised British Steel Corporation, and in turn during the early 1980s, part of the French, Pont-a-Mouson Group. Finally it was part of Saint Gobain as, in 2008, the works closed. The Avonside Engine Co. delivered 0-6-0ST, *Stanton 16*, new to Stanton in 1912, works no. 1617. Photographed on 14 August 1955, the engine moved to W. Ward Ltd, Eastwood (GN) Goods Yard, around June 1963, and was scrapped the following month.

Derbyshire, Stanton Iron Works, Ilkeston
Peckett's 0-6-0ST, works no. 1218, was delivered new to Market Overton Ironstone Quarries in 1910 and carried the name *Overton*. The engine moved to Stanton Ironworks, Derbyshire, in 1930, becoming *Stanton 28*. It was photographed on 14 August 1955 and went to Thos. W. Ward Ltd, Ilkeston, for scrap during December 1960.

Derbyshire, Stanton Iron Works, Ilkeston
Avonside 0-6-0ST, *Stanton no. 32*, is pictured on 14 August 1955. Whilst the name *Stanton 32* is quite clear on the photo, at one time this plate was indeed fitted to Hunslet 1853. It can only be assumed that at some time the plate was transferred to one of the Avonside locos.

Derbyshire, Stanton Iron Works, Ilkeston
Avonside delivered *Stanton 3* new to Stanton in 1909, works no.1567, when it was built.
Photographed on 14 August 1955, the engine was scrapped in 1965.

Derbyshire, Stanton Iron Works, Ilkeston
Avonside delivered 0-6-0ST, *Stanton no. 23*, new to Stanton in 1921, works no. 1882. Photographed
on 14 August1955, the engine was withdrawn in 1963 and scrapped around 1965.

Derbyshire, Stanton Iron Works, Ilkeston

Roger Hateley in *Railway Bylines March 2005* notes that between the mid 1930s and the 1950s, Stanton's fleet of conventional steam locomotives continued to increase, most of the new arrivals being products of Andrew Barclay. 0-6-0T, *Stanton no. 38* was delivered new by Andrew Barclay in 1949, works no. 2273. The engine was the last steam locomotive to be purchased new by the Stanton company. The standard Stanton corporate livery up to the 1970s was green, with white-black lining out. *Stanton no. 38* was scrapped on site by Thos. W. Ward Ltd, Sheffield, in September 1967.

Derbyshire, Stanton Iron Works, Staveley

0-4-0ST, *Lily*, built by Markham of Chesterfield in 1909 – no works number known – was delivered new to Stanton. The locomotive went to Steel Breaking & Dismantling Co. Ltd, Chesterfield, in November 1960.

Derbyshire, Stanton Iron Works, Staveley

The Staveley Coal & Iron Company Limited was based in Staveley, near Chesterfield, North Derbyshire. It exploited local ironstone quarried from land owned by the Duke of Devonshire on the outskirts of the village. It developed into coal mining, owning several collieries, and also into chemical production, first from those available from coal tar distillation, and later to cover a wide and diverse range. In 1960 the Staveley Iron & Chemical Company, which had been taken over by Stewarts & Lloyds Limited, was merged with the Ilkeston-based Stanton Iron Works to form Stanton & Staveley Ltd. *Bagnall no. 12*, works no. 2822, was built in 1945 and delivered new to Stanton. The engine was scrapped there in August 1971.

Derbyshire Stone Quarries, Matlock

The Matlock Derbyshire Stone quarries were situated adjacent to the railway station. Peckett 0-4-0ST, works no. 1749, was built in 1928 and delivered new to Matlock. Photographed in May 1970, the locomotive was acquired for preservation around May 1971 – originally at W. Roberts, Hill Farm, Tollerton, Notts., but is currently at the Lincolnshire Wolds Railway, Ludborough, Lincs.

Derbyshire Stone Quarries, Matlock

Peckett's 0-4-0ST, works no. 1555, was delivered new in 1920. The engine was loaned out between 1936 and 1947, and photographed in May 1970. In preservation, the loco moved to Riber Castle, Matlock, in July 1970.

Derbyshire, Derbyshire Stone Quarries, Wirksworth

Quarrying on the site dates from around 1830, and in time, the business traded as Bowne & Shaw. Stanton Ironworks bought a 50 per cent share in the company in 1921. After initially being served by Cromford Wharf, the quarries were connected to an extension of the Midland Railway's Wirksworth branch. Bowne & Shaw existed until December 1965 when the business became Derbyshire Stone Quarries, ending around 1970. Rail traffic came to an end by July 1991. 0-4-0DM, works no. 3357, was supplied new to Ind Coope Ltd by E. E. Baguley Ltd in 1952, where it became no. 1. It moved to Derbyshire Stone Quarries in March 1970, and the photograph was taken in the same year with the locomotive still displaying the Ind Coope name and logo. September 1990 saw a move to Chinnor & Princes Risborough Railway Association, Chinnor Cement Works, Chinnor, Oxfordshire. The locomotive is currently with the Devon Railway Centre, Tiverton.

Derbyshire, Derbyshire Stone Quarries, Wirksworth

Holwell no. 3, 0-4-0ST, moved to Wirksworth from Harlaxton Ironstone Quarries during August 1946. Built by Black, Hawthorne & Co. Ltd in 1873, the loco was delivered new to contractor Walter Scott and also spent time at South Witham Lime Quarries, Froddingham Iron & Steel Ltd, Coslterworth East Mines and Holwell Ironworks. *Holwell no. 3* was a typical Black Hathorn design with a short flat-sided saddle tank and spring balance safety valves mounted over the firebox. The engine was rebuilt in November 1894, November 1901, January 1912 and February 1935. For a time it also carried the name *Louis*. Clive Baker in *Railway Bylines* of January 2010 informs that the 'extension to the right hand side curved weatherboard was added at Wirksworth in 1948.' The chimney was a product of Holwell Ironworks; the original one would have featured a flared top. Photographed in June 1970, *Holwell no. 3* moved to the Tanfield Railway Co., Marley Hill, Co. Durham, on 19 November 1977, where it is known as *Wellington*.

Derbyshire, Derbyshire Stone Quarries, Wirksworth
4wDM, works no. 1470, was ex-Caldon Low Quarry, Staffordshire, before moving to Wirksworth in April 1970. Built by Kent Construction & Engine Co. in 1925, the engine was photographed on 4 September 1971. By July 1993, it had moved to Shropshire Loco Collection, Shropshire.

Derbyshire, Derbyshire Stone Quarries, Wirksworth
Uppingham moved to Wirksworth from Market Overton Quarries, Rutland, in September 1947. Built by Peckett in 1912, works no. 1257, the 0-4-0ST was delivered new to Uppingham Ironstone Quarries. The engine also saw service at Holwell Iron Works and was rebuilt in 1931/1932. Photographed in September 1971, *Uppingham* moved to the Midland Railway Co. Ltd, Derby, on 8 June 1974, but is currently located at Rocks by Rail, Cottesmore.

Chapter 2

Durham to Monmouthshire

Durham, Beamish Museum

Beamish Museum is located near the town of Stanley, County Durham. The museum's guiding principle is to preserve an example of everyday life in urban and rural North East England at the climax of industrialisation in the early twentieth century. 0-4-0 vertical-boiler locomotive, affectionately nicknamed 'The Coffee Pot', was built by Head Wrightson & Co. in 1871 for the Dorking Greystone Lime Company. It was fitted with sprung buffers and a 300-gallon water tank instead of a more standard 150-gallon version. By the early 1950s it was redundant; in September 1960 it was re-purchased by its makers who by then had become Head Wrightson Teasdale Ltd. After some restoration The Coffee Pot was offered to Beamish in 1962, but did not move there until 1970. It is seen here in 1986 after undergoing one of many refurbishments whilst at the museum.

Durham, Beamish Museum
In 'Seaham Harbour and its Railways', *Railway Bylines* (September 2002), Steven Oakden states that Seaham Harbour, roughly midway between Sunderland and Hartlepool on the County Durham coast, had one of the best-known and best-loved industrial railway systems in the country. 0-4-0 well tank locomotive no. 18 was built by Stephen Lewin of Poole in 1877 (or so it is believed) as an 0-4-0 well tank and acquired by Seaham in 1899. Later, it was rebuilt in the company's workshops, firstly as a side tank, and in 1927, as a saddle tank. Oakden adds that the Lewin was regarded by the crews as a good little engine, but it was condemned in the early 1970s. By January 1975, no. 18 had been taken to Beamish Museum for preservation where it is seen here, restored to its original condition with a well tank and no cab.

Opposite above: Durham, Tanfield Railway
The Tanfield Railway is a standard-gauge heritage railway in Gateshead and County Durham. Running on part of a former colliery's wooden wagonway, later a steam railway, it operates preserved steam and diesel industrial tank locomotives. The railway operates a passenger service on Sundays all year round, as well as demonstration freight trains. The line runs 3 miles between a southern terminus at East Tanfield, Durham, to a northern terminus at Sunniside, Gateshead, with the main station, Andrews House, situated near to the Marley Hill engine shed. No. 21, 0-4-0ST, built by Robert Stephenson & Hawthorns in 1954, was formerly owned by the Central Electricity Generating Board and used for shunting purposes at the pair of coal-fired Stella power stations in the North East. The engine is presently stored awaiting overhaul at the Tanfield Railway where it was photographed in August 1978.

Opposite below: Durham, Tanfield Railway
0-4-0ST, NCB no. 32, built by Andrew Barclay in 1920, works no. 1659, is currently undergoing restoration at the Tanfield where it is seen at the Marley Hill shed on 9 July 1978.

Essex, East Anglian Railway Museum, Chappel and Wakes Colne Station
Stewarts & Lloyds (Minerals) bought no. 2350 *Belvoir*, built by Andrew Barclay in 1954, for use on their Harston site. In fact the locomotive was named after the nearby Belvoir Castle and spent its working life in that area. When steam became redundant as part of the contraction of the ironstone quarrying industry in the late 1960s and early 1970s, *Belvoir* went to the East Anglian Railway Museum at Chappel & Wakes Colne Station. It was pictured there in May 1972. More recently, the locomotive was donated to the Rutland Railway Museum at Cottesmore by a private collector.

Glamorgan, Mountain Ash
Andrew Barclay's 0-6-0ST *Llantarnam Abbey*, works no. 2074, is seen here on the Mountain Ash railway system in April 1976. In *Industrial Locomotives of Mid & South Glamorgan* (2007), Geoffrey Hill traces some of the locomotive's history: it was ex-Penrikyber Colliery by September 1957, then Merthyr Valle Colliery by June 1960, ex-Aberaman Railways by September 1964, Mountain Ash Central Workshops by February 1970, it then moved to Walkden Central Workshops, Lancashire, in May 1971, and then returned to Mountain Ash, where it was incorrectly named *Llantanam Abbey*, in September 1971. The spelling was rectified at Mountain Ash after April 1973. It is also mentioned that the locomotive went to Lower Swansea Valley Railway Preservation Society for preservation. The locomotive is currently at the Pontypool & Blaenavon Railway.

Gwynedd, Bala Lake

The Bala Lake Railway is a preserved railway at Bala Lake, Gwynedd, North Wales. Hunslet 0-4-0ST, works no. 822, was built in 1903, and was subsequently named after a racehorse, *Maid Marian*. The engine spent its entire industrial life working at the Dinorwic Slate Quarry in North Wales. It was withdrawn in 1964 and a year later a group of enthusiasts formed the Maid Marian Locomotive Fund and bought the locomotive for preservation. *Maid Marian* operated at the Bressingham Steam Museum from 1967 to 1971, before going to the Llanberis Lake Railway until 1975, and then to Bala Lake.

Hampshire, Woolmer Instructional Military Railway, later Longmoor Military Railway

Gazelle emerged from A. Dodman & Co. Ltd, Highgate Works, Kings Lynn, in 1893, as a 2-2-2 well tank. It was built for William Burkett, a businessman with considerable influence with certain railway companies, who used the engine for local business trips. In 1911 it was converted to an 0-4-2 well tank by Colonel Stephens for use on the Shropshire & Montgomeryshire Railway. Transferred to Longmoor and displayed outside the camp, *Gazelle* is pictured here in October 1968. When Longmoor closed, *Gazelle* was moved to the National Railway Museum.

Hampshire, Woolmer Instructional Military Railway, later Longmoor Military Railway
The Woolmer Instructional Military Railway in Hampshire was built by the Royal Engineers in order to train soldiers on railway construction and operations. The railway was re-laid to 4-ft-8½-in.-(1,435-mm) standard gauge in 1905-07, and renamed the Longmoor Military Railway in 1935. Andrew Barclay 0-4-0ST no. 1398 *Lord Fisher* was built in 1915 and on 7 September of that year went to the Royal Naval Airship Station near Rochester in Kent. After being used at a number of MOD and private locations, it was withdrawn in May 1967. Early in the following year it arrived at Longmoor together with other preserved locomotives. *Lord Fisher* was the last engine to work on the Longmoor Military Railway system being employed in the clearing up operation after the filming of the Columbia Pictures' movie, *Young Winston*. It was photographed at Longmoor in October 1968 but is presently housed at the East Somerset Railway, Cranmore. The locomotive is currently in regular use as shed pilot and on 'Driver-for-a-Fiver' footplate courses.

Opposite above: Hampshire, Woolmer Instructional Military Railway, later Longmoor Military Railway
0-6-0ST *Woolmer*, works no. 1572, was erected in 1910 by the Avonside Engine C. Ltd, Bristol for the Woolmer Instructional Military Railway. The engine worked until 1954 and is seen there in October 1968. Longmoor Military Railway closed down with a ceremonial last day of operation on 31 October 1969. *Woolmer* is currently on loan from the NRM to the Milestones Living History Museum, Hampshire.

Opposite below: Hampshire, Woolmer Instructional Military Railway later Longmoor Military Railway
Sentinel/Rolls Royce 0-8-0 diesel-hydraulic no. 890 *General Lord Robertson* was delivered to Longmoor in 1963 and is pictured there in October 1968. The locomotive was later renumbered 610, and moved to MOD Shoeburyness when the LMR closed in 1969. Since 1986 *General Lord Robertson* has been at the Avon Valley Railway.

Hertfordshire, The Knebworth & Winter Green Railway
The Knebworth & Winter Green Railway was a narrow-gauge railway built in 1972 in the grounds of Knebworth House by Pleasurerail Ltd, a company set up to build and operate private tourist railways. 0-4-0VBT *Chaloner*, seen at Knebworth, is an example of De Winton & Co.'s distinctive vertical boiler deigns. The engine was built in 1877 and worked on the 2-ft-gauge lines in the Pen-y-Bryn slate quarry, moving to Pen-yr-Orsedd nearby in 1888. Sold to a private collector in 1960, *Chaloner* is now preserved at the Leighton Buzzard Light Railway. All the photographs in this Knebworth section were taken by Bill Reed in September 1978.

Hertfordshire, The Knebworth & Winter Green Railway
During its existence, the K&WGR line hosted a number of steam and diesel locomotives. The line continued to run until 1990 when it was lifted and the remaining stock transferred to other preservation railways. Hunslet 0-4-0ST, works no. 1429, *Lady Joan* was built in 1922 and was used on slate quarries in North Wales until 1967. The engine spent time at Knebworth and Woburn before being acquired by the Bredgar & Wormshill Light Railway in 1996.

Hertfordshire, The Knebworth & Winter Green Railway
Built in 1915 by the Avonside Locomotive Company, works no. 1738, 0-4-0T locomotive, *Sezela* no. 4 was originally supplied to the sugar cane railway of Reynolds Brothers, Sezela, Natal, South Africa. It was one of six similar locomotives and remained in South Africa until 1971. Brought back to England in the following year, the engine was restored and kept at the K&WGR. In 1990, *Sezela* was sold to the Bygone Heritage Village Museum, Great Yarmouth. It went to the West Highland Railway Porthmadog on 3 September 1994, and by 1997, it had been overhauled and was in working order. Unofficially known as *Ivor*, the engine is now resident at the Leighton Buzzard Light Railway.

Hertfordshire, The Knebworth & Winter Green Railway
Kerr Stuart & Co.'s 0-4-0ST 'Wren' class locomotive, 4256 *Peter Pan*, dates from 1922. Of the several standard types of industrial locomotives built by KS & Co., the 'Wren' was the smallest in size yet the most numerous. *Peter Pan* worked on various contracts from new, before being sold to Devon County Council in 1929 and based at Wilminstone Quarry near Tavistock. It is currently based at the Leighton Buzzard Light Railway.

Opposite above: Hertfordshire, The Knebworth & Winter Green Railway
W. G. Bagnall's 0-4-0ST, works no. 2090, was built in 1919 and named *Pixie*. The engine worked for some years in the Cranford iron ore quarries before being acquired in 1962 by the Revd Teddy Boston who established the Cadeby Light Railway in the garden of his rectory near Market Bosworth, Leics. The locomotive is currently at a private location.

Opposite below: Hertfordshire, The Knebworth & Winter Green Railway
Peckett & Sons' 0-6-0ST 2-ft-gauge no. 1270 *Triassic* was built in 1911. Delivered to Kay & Co.'s lime and cement works, Warwickshire, the engine spent all of its industrial life there. Five of Kay & Co.'s Pecketts were named after types of rock and the sixth was named after its regular driver. Writer J. B. Latham bought *Triassic* in 1957 and moved the loco to his home at Woking. The engine was at Knebworth between 1972 and the late 1980s, before moving to the Leighton Buzzard narrow-gauge railway, and becoming a resident at Bala Lake in 1992. In subsequent years *Triassic* has spent time at the Ffestiniog railway and the NRM.

Above: Hertfordshire, The Knebworth & Winter Green Railway
Hunslet 0-4-0ST *Lilla*, works no. 554, built in 1891, formerly worked in the slate quarries of North Wales. The locomotive arrived at Knebworth in 1972, but is now based on the Ffestiniog Railway. *Lilla* is cared for by the Lilla Locomotive Group who run 'drive-an-engine' experience runs, slate shunts and corporate training days. On www.festiniograilway.org.uk it is stated, 'Hunslets had carved a niche, specializing in industrial and narrow-gauge engines, having a "special relationship" with the Welsh quarries supplying 50 similar locomotives between 1870 and 1932 ... Although the basic design was similar, there were detail variations and *Lilla* is unique. The Chief Draughtsman was probably Arthur Hird. *Lilla's* work began at Cilgwyn Slate Quarry in the Nantlle Valley, Gwynedd. She is larger than most quarry engines.'

Opposite above: Hertfordshire, The Knebworth & Winter Green Railway
Sao Domingo, an Orenstein & Koppel 0-6-0 well tank, works no. 11784, was built in 1925. The engine was on site at Knebworth in 1979 but on static display only. It moved to South Tynedale Railway in 1980, and is now restored to working order at the Great Bush Railway, a private 2-ft-gauge railway running round the edge of Tinker's Park, Hadlow Down, Sussex. Orenstein & Koppel was a major German engineering company specialising in railway vehicles, escalators, and heavy equipment. It was founded on 1 April 1876 in Berlin by Benno Orenstein and Arthur Koppel. O&K pulled out of the railway business in 1981.

Opposite below: Highland Aviemore
Andrew Barclay 0-4-0ST 2073 *Dailuaine Distillery no.1* was built in 1939. It is pictured at Aviemore shed in June 1978. On www.singlemaltsdirect.com it states, '[The] Dailuaine [distillery founded in 1852 by William Mackenzie] was connected to the Strathspey railway line for more than a century and had its own steam locomotive, *Dailuaine no. 1*, which carried supplies to and from the distillery. It was in use until 1967.' The locomotive is currently located at the Strathspey Railway Aviemore, Highland, awaiting restoration. The company's main workshop is at Aviemore and housed in the original Highland Railway locomotive engine shed, built in 1897.

Above: Kent, Sittingbourne and Kemsley Light Railway
The Sittingbourne & Kemsley Light Railway is a 2-ft-6-in.-(762-mm) gauge heritage railway that operates from Sittingbourne to the banks of the Swale. The line was formerly owned by Bowater, the paper making firm, and was used to carry raw materials and finished products between Ridham Dock and the company's two mills, one at Sittingbourne and the other at Kemsley. In the late 1960s the railway faced closure by its owners but the Locomotive Club of Great Britain accepted an offer to operate the railway from 1970. Seen here on 12 August 1970 is Bagnall 2-4-0 narrow-gauge fireless locomotive, *Unique*, works no. 2216, built in 1924. The engine is currently on static display at Kemsley Down Station. Steam was provided from an external source, and stored on the 'fireless' locomotive in a well-insulated pressure vessel. Such locomotives were useful when working around inflammable materials.

Kent, Sittingbourne and Kemsley Light Railway
Bagnall's 0-6-2T, *Triumph*, works no. 2511, built in 1934, was photographed at Sittingbourne Station on 12 August 1970. At its peak the S&K railway used twelve conventional steam locos, as well as two fireless locomotives, one battery electric locomotive and an oil engine internal combustion loco.

Kent, Sittingbourne and Kemsley Light Railway
The Bowaters Paper Railway had the distinction of being the last steam-operated industrial narrow-gauge railway in Britain when it closed in 1969. The first use of steam locomotives on the railway came in 1905, the same year that two 0-4-2T locomotives were obtained from Kerr Stuart, their *Brazil* class. They were originally numbered 1 and 2, but later named *Premier* and *Leader* respectively. Kerr Stuart 0-4-2ST *Leader*, works no. 926, is depicted here. It is noticeable that the round saddle tank covers only the boiler barrel and does not have a dome. A few years after it was built, the engine was rebuilt, as was its sister, *Premier*.

Kent, Sittingbourne and Kemsley Light Railway

Kerr Stuart's 0-4-2ST *Premier* of 1905, works no. 886, is seen at Kemsley Sidings, Sittinghbourne, in August 1970. In 2008-09, the preserved line survived a threat of closure due to the owners of Sittingbourne Paper Mill closing the mill and selling the land. Also the lease held by the railway expired in January 2009. Negotiations resulted in the railway being saved, although no public trains ran in 2009.

Kent, Sittingbourne and Kemsley Light Railway

Bagnall-built 0-6-2T *Alpha*, works no. 2472, in 1932. The majority of Bagnall's products were small four- and six-coupled steam locomotives for industrial use, and many were narrow gauge. The company introduced several novel types of locomotive valve gear, including the Bagnall-Price and the Baguley. They also used marine (circular) fireboxes on narrow-gauge engines, a design that was cheap but needed a different firing technique. Interestingly, some of Kerr Stuart's designs were brought to Bagnall's when they employed Kerr Stuart's chief draughtsman.

Kent, Sittingbourne and Kemsley Light Railway

Kerr Stuart's 0-4-2ST *Melior*, works no. 4219, was built in 1924. The engine is pictured at Sittingbourne during October 1970. The *Brazil* class of locomotives was initially built by Kerr Stuart, but later the design was taken over by Hunslet. The locomotives were built to a variety of gauges from 2 ft up to 4 ft 8½ in.

Lancashire, Steamtown Carnforth

Steamtown was the name for the former British Rail 10A engine shed, sidings, carriage and wagon works west of Carnforth railway station. It opened to the public in 1969 and developed into a major tourist attraction. Bagnall 0-6-0ST *Cranford no.2*, works no. 2668, was built in 1942 with 15-in. cylinders. It was one of a batch of six built for use in the limestone quarries in Northamptonshire and Oxfordshire. *Cranford no. 2* was delivered new to Cranford Ironstone Company, Northants, being their no. 2 – an older engine there was named *Cranford*. When preserved, the loco was initially based at Carnforth, but later it moved to the Embsay & Bolton Abbey Steam Railway where, following much work, it became one of their main engines.

Lancashire, Steamtown Carnforth

0-6-0 fireless locomotive, works no. 3019, was ordered from Bagnall's in September 1949 by Shell Refining and Marketing Co. Ltd. The loco was delivered in May 1952 to Trimpell Ltd (a subsidiary company) of Heysham, Lancashire, and numbered 5. The engine was sold in November 1970 to Lakeside Railway and put in their museum at Carnforth. Six Bagnall fireless locomotives have been preserved in Great Britain. This is a surprisingly large number since Bagnall's built only fourteen fireless locomotives in total.

Lancashire, Steamtown Carnforth

Sentinel 0-4-0VBT *Gasbag*, works no. 8024, was built in 1929 and spent most of its working life with the Gas Board in Cambridge. In preservation, the engine moved to Steamtown Carnforth where it became a regular, in use for shunting and demonstration trains. Photographed in September 1969, the locomotive is currently located at the Ribble Steam Railway, Preston.

Above: Lancashire, Lytham Motive Power Museum
In *Old Glory Vintage Restoration Today* No. 27 (May 1992), Tony Peart states that Jim Morris's Lytham Motive Power Museum 'was established about a quarter of a century ago in his Helical Springs factory in Lytham.' The collection grew rapidly and, in 1969, the museum was opened to the public in a purpose-built roundhouse, while a narrow-gauge railway was laid outside. In 1992, Jim decided to retire and the main contents of his collection were sold on 1 March of that year. Tony Peart pointed out that an undoubted gem amongst Jim's locomotives was Neilson & Company's 0-4-0 narrow-gauge crane tank, works no. 4004. It left Springburn Works in 1890 to become locomotive no. 6 of the Hodbarrow hematite mines, near Millom in Cumberland. The engine was known as 'Snipey' – as the crane resembled the beak of a marshland dwelling snipe – and was first preserved at Lytham Motive Power Museum during the early 1970s. The photograph was taken in October 1969. Apparently the locomotive remains privately owned and out of public view, but safe.

Opposite above: Lancashire, Lytham Motive Power Museum
Bagnall 0-6-0ST *Princess*, works no. 2682, built in 1942, is pictured at Lytham during September 1969. The loco has since become part of the Lakeside & Haverthwaite Railway (a heritage railway in Cumbria) where it is operational, painted in dark blue and lined out in black and red. The railway's website adds the following information: '*Princess* was the prototype of a small class of powerful shunting engines produced by W. G. Bagnall & Co. Ltd, of Stafford, capable of developing tractive effort of 22,382 lbs. *Princess* is unusual for an industrial type of locomotive in that it is fitted with steam heating apparatus, the reason for this being it was used for warming the vans of the Geest Company's bananas imported from the West Indies, the maintenance of correct storage temperatures being critical.'

Opposite below: Lancashire, Lytham Motive Power Museum
Vulcan Foundry's 0-4-0ST *Vulcan*, works no. 3272, built in 1918, is pictured at Lytham in October 1978. The locomotive is currently located at Barrow Hill, Staveley.

Leicestershire, Castle Donnington
Castle Donnington Power Station was built in 1959 at a cost of £30 million. At the time it was the largest in Western Europe, and from the outset, steam locomotives were employed for internal shunting and they were kept in perfect condition. Two identical 0-6-0ST locomotives were supplied by Robert Stephenson & Hawthorns. *Castle Donington Power Station no. 1*, works no. 7817, built in 1954, worked at the power station until the latter's closure. Since moving to the Midland Railway, Butterley, the engine has received a full overhaul funded by the European Union Culture 2000 scheme through the Steam Rail Net partnership. Vacuum brakes and a steam heating system have been fitted to allow passenger train operation. The photograph was taken at the power station in August 1971.

Leicestershire, Donisthorpe Colliery

Donisthorpe Colliery near Ashby-De-La-Zouch, Leicestershire, was first sunk in 1871 by the colliery owners Checkland & Williams to a depth of 205 m (672 feet). In 1890 they deepened mine to 263 m (863 feet). The colliery was situated north of Donnisthorpe railway station, and sidings connected to the rail network via a branch running west from the Ashby & Nuneaton Joint Railway line. Rail traffic had ceased by July 1980 and the colliery itself closed in March 1990. *Snibston no. 1*, 0-4-0DH, works no. 434024, was built by Ruston & Hornsby Ltd in 1961. The engine was delivered new to Snibston Colliery, moving to Donnisthorpe Colliery during February 1965. Photographed in May 1971, *Snibston no. 1* was exported to Belgium on 17 November 1980.

Leicestershire, Shackerstone Railway Society Ltd (The Battlefield Line), Market Bosworth
The society operates the railway from Shackerstone Station, via Market Bosworth, to Shenton, the site of the famous Battle of Bosworth in 1485. Hunslet 0-4-0ST, works no. 1493, built in 1925, was supplied new to Pye Hill Colliery (ex-James Oakes & Co, Riddings Collieries Ltd) in Nottinghamshire. The engine moved to Moor Green Central Workshops on several occasions and returned each time to Pye Hill, before moving to Shackerstone on 27 November 1971. Photographed during April 1974, the engine is currently located at the Middleton Railway.

Leicestershire, Holwell Ironworks, Melton Mowbray
The Holwell Ironworks & Foundry was sited at the junction of the Melton Mowbray – Nottingham line and was established by December 1881. The company was styled Holwell Ironworks Ltd until January 1918, then Holwell Ironworks & Foundry and later – from 2005 – it came under the Saint Gobain Pipelines. The works were connected to a branch which extended north-east from the Midland Railway's Mowbray to Nottingham line. Rail traffic came to a halt in 1995. Hawthorne Leslie's 0-4-0ST no. 2, works no. 2458, was built in 1900 and delivered new to Holwell. Photographed in May 1970, the engine was scrapped on site by F. Berry Ltd, Leicester, in February 1971.

Leicestershire, Holwell Ironworks, Melton Mowbray
Hudswell Clarke's 0-4-0ST *Holwell no. 15,* works no. 1321, was built in 1917 and delivered new to Holwell. The engine was rebuilt in 1950 and photographed in May 1970. It was scrapped on site by F. Barry Ltd, Leicester February 1971.

Leicestershire, Holwell Ironworks, Melton Mowbray
0-4-0ST *Stanton 18*, built by A. Barclay, works no. 1791, in 1923 was delivered new to Holwell. Photographed during May 1970, the engine was scrapped in 1973.

Lincolnshire, Harlaxton Ironstone Quarries

A standard-gauge system was built at Harlaxton by Stanton Ironworks Co. Ltd in 1940/41 to meet the demand for iron ore during the Second World War. The complex included marshalling yards, workshops and a locomotive shed. Stewarts & Lloyds took over from January 1950 and then British Steel Corporation – Tubes Division, Minerals – from March 1970. The workings were closed in February 1974 and the track was lifted. Operations resumed on a small scale in April 1976 until March 1977. The output in this latter period was transported by lorry to a tipping dock at Casthorpe. Andrew Barclay built 0-6-0T *Ajax* in 1918, works no. 1605. It became a much travelled locomotive having been with George Cohen, Sons & Co. Ltd, Holwell Ironworks, Woolsthorpe Quarries and Buckminster Quarries, before moving to Harlaxton in August 1955 where it was photographed on 1 October 1967. During November 1972, the engine went to Wight Locomotive Society, Haven Street Station, Isle of Wight.

Opposite above: Lincolnshire, Harlaxton Ironstone Quarries
Denton was delivered new to Woolsthorpe Ironstone Quarries by Barclay's in 1951, works no. 2306. The 0-6-0ST moved to Harlaxton in October 1962 but returned to Woolsthorpe during March 1964. A final move to Harlaxton occurred on 3 April 1967 where the engine was photographed in August of that year. *Denton* was scrapped during October 1969.

Opposite below: Lincolnshire, Harlaxton Ironstone Quarries
Rutland, a large 0-6-0ST, was built by Andrew Barclay in 1954, works no. 2351. The engine was delivered new to Market Overton Ironstone Quarries and moved to Woolsthorpe Quarries, Leicestershire, during May 1967. The transfer to Harlaxton occurred in January 1964 where the engine was photographed on 1 October 1967. *Rutland* was scrapped on site by Thomas W. Ward Ltd in November 1969.

Monmouthshire, Big Pit Blaenavon
Andrew Barclay's 0-4-0ST *Nora No.5*, built in 1912, is pictured at the Big Pit Blaenavon in April 1976. The mine was situated about a mile north of the ex-LNWR High Level railway station and was served by what became familiarly known as the Blaenavon Railways. This was an extensive system which had been developed to serve the Blaenavon Iron & Steel Company, and its many collieries and coke ovens. After working a lifetime in the area, *Nora no. 5* is now a static exhibit at the Welsh Mining Museum, which is housed at the old Big Pit Colliery that closed in 1980.

Chapter 3
Norfolk to Nottinghamshire

Norfolk, Bressingham
Bressingham Steam Museum and Garden is the brainchild of gardener Allan Bloom, who created an unusual combination of historic railway and horticultural delight. There are 5 miles of narrow-gauge railway track – and four different gauge tracks. Over forty steam locomotives are on view, plus traction and stationary engines. NG Hunslet 0-4-0ST *Gwynedd* was built in 1883, works no. 316, and worked in the Penrhyn slate quarries. The engine was repainted in 2000 in its original 1883 livery by the Festiniog Railway when it returned to North Wales for the first time in thirty-five years. The photograph dates from June 1974.

Norfolk, Bressingham

Ex-NCB Beyer-Garratt 0-4-0 + 0-4-0 *William Francis*, built by Beyer Peacock in 1937, works no. 6841, was photographed in July 1975. The locomotive was formerly based at Baddesley Colliery, Baxterley, Warwickshire, where it was used primarily to haul coal trains between the colliery and the exchange sidings at Atherstone.

Norfolk, the North Norfolk Railway

The North Norfolk Railway – the 'Poppy Line' – is a heritage steam railway, running between Sheringham and Holt. Over the years, several locomotives have been based on the line before moving on to alternative locations. One example is 0-6-0ST *Ashington no.5*. Built by Peckett and Sons Ltd. in 1939, works no. 1979, the engine went to the Ashington Coal Company, Northumberland, spending its entire industrial career there. In 1969 the loco was sold by the NCB to the NNR. However, a return to Northumberland occurred in 1991 and *no.5* was named 'Jackie Milburn' in honour of the local football hero. The loco was photographed at Sherringham Station in July 1977.

Northamptonshire, Corby District Council, West Glebe Park
Hawthorne Leslie's 0-6-0ST, built in 1934, works no. 3827, was delivered new to Corby Works, becoming no. 14. The engine was moved to Corby Town Council, West Glebe Park, for preservation during September 1971. On 11 January 1989 it was taken to the Vic Berry Company Ltd, Leicester, for asbestos removal and then to East Carlton Countryside Park. The loco was photographed on 26 January 1974.

Northamptonshire, Corby & District Model Railway Society exhibit, West Glebe Park, Corby
Hunslet's 0-6-0ST, works no. 2411, was erected in 1941 and delivered new to Corby Works, becoming no. 24. The locomotive was preserved as a static exhibit in West Glebe Park between October 1973 and 1980 when the loco was moved to Market Overton Industrial Railway Association, Rutland. Photographed in West Glebe Park on 26 January 1974, the engine is currently located at Swindon & Cricklade Railway Society.

Northamptonshire, Corby Works
D10, 0-6-0DH, was supplied new to Stewarts & Lloyds Ltd by the North British Locomotive Company, Glasgow, in 1962, works no. 28052. Photographed on 26 January 1974, it was scrapped on site by Shanks & McEwan (England) Ltd in August 1982.

Northamptonshire, Corby Works
Rolls Royce, Sentinel Works, Shrewsbury, built D39 (formerly D23, *John*) 0-4-0DH in 1965, works no. 10206. Ex-Oxfordshire Ironstone Co. Ltd, the engine arrived at British Steel, Corby Works, on 23 October 1967. The picture was taken on 26 January 1974 and the locomotive went to Thomas Hill (Rotherham) Ltd, Vanguard Works, Kilnhurst, South Yorkshire, for resale on 4 July 1977.

Northamptonshire, Corby Works
D40 (formerly D24 *Allan*) was ex-Oxfordshire Ironstone Co. Ltd before arrival at British Steel in October 1967. It was built by Rolls Royce, Sentinel Works, Shrewsbury, in 1965, works no. 10208, and is pictured on 26 January 1974. The locomotive went to Thomas Hill (Rotherham) Ltd, Vanguard Works, Kilnhurst, South Yorkshire, for resale on 15 July 1977.

Northamptonshire, Corby Works
D25, 0-6-0DH, was supplied new by English Electric, Vulcan Works, in 1971, works no. 5356. The photograph was taken on 26 January 1974 and the locomotive was scrapped on site by Shanks & McEwan (England) Ltd, in August 1982.

Northamptonshire, Corby Works

Dolobran was supplied new by Manning Wardle to Lloyds Ironstone Co. Ltd in 1910 (controlled by Stewarts & Lloyds from 1923), works no. 1762. The engine was transferred to Stewarts & Lloyds Minerals Ltd, Corby, during November 1949. Photographed in 1969, the engine moved to Tenterden Railway Co. Ltd, Rolvenden, Kent, on 19 August 1972. From there it went to Woolwich before being moved to Peak Rail in Derbyshire in 2002, and to Ruddington in 2003 for restoration to working order.

Northamptonshire, Corby Works

Stewarts & Lloyds Corby had the distinction of operating locomotives to the above design by three successive manufacturers. Manning Wardle supplied examples in 1910, while Kitsons supplied a further seven in the 1930s. In 1940 Robert Stephenson & Hawthorns, who had in turn acquired the patterns, produced a further five locomotives with little change in the original design. The locomotives featured 16 x 22-in cylinders and 3-ft-6-in-diameter wheels. Kitson's 0-6-0ST, works no. 5470, no. 45 *Colwyn*, built in 1933 was photographed at Corby Works in 1969. The engine is currently preserved at the Northampton Steam Railway.

Northamptonshire, Corby Works

0-6-0ST *Carnarvon* arrived new from Kitsons to Stewarts & Lloyds Ltd in 1933, works no. 5474. The engine became part of Stewarts & Lloyds Minerals Ltd, Corby, in November 1949 and was photographed in 1969. On 11 October 1969 the loco went to the Worcester Locomotive Society and was used on the Severn Valley Railway that year. This was followed by a move to the Bulmers Railway Centre in Hereford in 1970, and it was even used for shunting Bulmer's freight trains during an oil shortage in 1973. In 1993 it moved to the South Devon Railway.

Northamptonshire, Corby Quarries

The loco has S&L Minerals on the cab side in this photograph taken in 1969. But Stewarts & Lloyds Minerals Ltd had ceased by 1 July 1968 in favour of British Steel Corporation, Northern & Tubes Group (existing until 23 March 1970). The engine was built by Robert Stephenson & Hawthorns, Newcastle-upon-Tyne, in 1950, works no. 7667, and supplied new to S&L, becoming no. 56. During September 1972, the locomotive went to Tenterden Railway Co. Ltd, Rolvenden, Kent, but is currently with the Great Central Railway (Nottingham) Ltd.

Opposite above: Northamptonshire, Corby Works
No. 16 (formerly S&L no. 11), 0-6-0ST, was built by Hawthorne Leslie & Co. in 1934, works no. 3837, and supplied new to S&L Ltd. Photographed on 26 January 1974, during June of that year the engine went to the Peterborough Locomotive Society, Cambridge, but is now with the Lavender Line Preservation Society, Uckfield. The following information is on the society's website: 'This 0-6-0ST has been rescued by the Hawthorne & Leslie Preservation Society as a long term project to bring her back to steam after standing for 25 years at the Leatherhead Leisure centre.'

Opposite below: Northamptonshire, Glendon Sidings
Ex-BR Type 1 Class 14, D9523 0-6-0DH, was built at Swindon Works in 1964. It was ex-Hull Dairycoates and Corby Quarries and was photographed at Glendon Sidings in 1969. In December 1980 it moved to the old Bessemer Plant for storage. On 16 October 1981 the engine went to the Great Central Railway (1976) Ltd, but has since moved to the Derwent Valley Light Railway.

Above: Northamptonshire, Kettering
The Kettering Iron Ore Co. began quarrying for ironstone in an area north-west of Kettering Station from 1870. Standard-gauge sidings and locomotives were used at the furnaces, whilst a 3-ft-gauge tramway connected the quarries with the iron works. Furnaces were also built on the site in 1878 and 1889. After 21 April 1876, the business was styled Kettering Iron & Coal Ltd/Kettering Furnaces & Quarries and from October 1956 it was a subsidiary of Stewarts & Lloyds Ltd. The furnaces were dismantled by 1960, and quarrying had ceased by 1962. Manning Wardle 0-6-0ST, 3-ft-gauge no. 1675, *Kettering Furnaces no. 8*, was delivered new to the company in 1906. On 26 August 1963 the engine went to the Borough of Kettering, Manor House Grounds, for preservation. It is pictured there in February 1974, but is currently held by Welland Valley Vintage Traction Club, Market Harborough.

Northamptonshire, John R Billowes Ltd, Pytchley Road Industrial Estate, Kettering
Robin Wayell (2001) lists Billowes' site under the chapter heading 'Preservation Locations'. He also adds that 'preserved motive power' was kept there for a time. Ex-Stewarts & Lloyds Minerals Ltd no. 86, a Peckett 0-6-0ST 1871 of 1934, was photographed at the Billowes' site on 26 January 1974. The engine was one of two Pecketts supplied in 1934, and no. 86 was transferred to Billowes in June 1967, moving to Northamptonshire Ironstone Railway Trust Ltd, Northampton, on 10 June 1975.

Nottinghamshire, The Boots Co. Ltd, Beeston Works
Jesse Boot established his pharmaceutical company in Nottingham in 1888. Later the company opened a large works on a 340-acre site at Beeston, which had a sidings connecting with the Nottingham–Beeston line. Within the works there was also a 1-ft-8-in.-gauge line and a 2-ft gauge. The standard-gauge line had closed by May 1981. B7211, 0-4-0DE, was supplied new by Ruston & Hornsby Ltd, works no. 384139, in 1955. The engine moved to the Midland Railway Trust Ltd, Derbyshire, on 12 January 1982.

Nottinghamshire, The Boots Co. Ltd, Beeston Works
No. 2, 0-4-0F, was supplied new by A. Barclay in 1935, works no. 2008. The engine moved to the
Midland Railway Trust Ltd, Derbyshire, on 12 January 1982.

Nottinghamshire, Bentinck Colliery, Kirkby-in-Ashfield
Coal production had begun at the colliery by 1896 and it was connected to both the Midland
Railway and MS&LR (GCR) lines. There were also coke ovens and a brick works adjacent.
Bentinck no. 3 0-6-0ST was supplied new to the colliery by the Yorkshire Engine Co. Ltd, Sheffield,
in 1928, works no. 2197. The engine was moved to Brookhill loco shed in January 1967. The
introduction of BR trains loaded by a rapid loading bunker ended the work of NCB locomotives
in March 1982. Bentinck was merged with Annesley Colliery from March 1988 and continued to
be the coal outlet. In January 1999, it was announced that Midlands Mining PLC was intending
to close Annesley-Bentinck Colliery by the end of the year, due to geological problems and adverse
market conditions. The last shift was completed on Friday 28 January 2000.

Nottinghamshire, Bestwood Colliery

The colliery began production in 1876 and was connected initially to the Midland Railway's Bestwood Park branch line and later to the GN's Leen Valley line. 0-4-0ST *Lancaster* was supplied new to the colliery by Peckett & Sons in 1888, works no. 468. The locomotive was scrapped on site by Ilkeston Metal & Waste Co. Ltd in October 1964. The colliery closed in July 1967 and in the same decade one of the (ex-LNER) branch lines to the colliery and central workshops was closed; the ex-LMSR line was redundant by October 1971.

Nottinghamshire, Bestwood

Andrew Barclay's 0-4-0ST *Bestwood* dates from 1919, works no. 1517. The engine was ex-B.A. collieries and spent time at Calverton colliery during the early 1950s besides spells at Bestwood Central workshops. During the nationalisation period it was one of three 0-4-0STs at the colliery. Photographed in 1966, *Bestwood* was scrapped on site during July 1968.

Nottinghamshire, Bestwood

Markham & Co. Ltd of Chesterfield built 0-4-0ST *St Albans* in 1891, works no. 104, and the engine was supplied new to Bestwood Colliery. Markham & Co. were manufacturers of colliery winding machinery, but in 1889 they commenced steam locomotive production. Up to 1914, they built nineteen locomotives. A characteristic of their engines was the angular saddle tank with its multitude of round-headed rivets. Also favoured was the tapered chimney and safety valves which were set on a centrally mounted dome. *St Albans* was scrapped on site by the end of March 1956.

Nottinghamshire, Bestwood

Hawthorne Leslie's 0-6-0ST *Valerie* was built in 1924, works no. 3606. The engine was much travelled having previously worked at Holloway Bros (London) Ltd, Linby Colliery, Babbington Colliery, Calverton Colliery, and was ex-Bestwood Workshops before a second stint at Bestwood Colliery in October 1962. This was the only HL 0-6-0ST locomotive to work at Bestwood. Photographed during August, 1967, *Valerie* was scrapped on site during October 1969.

Nottinghamshire, Bestwood

When this picture was taken in August 1967, 0-6-0ST no. 3, *Felix* was only four years away from being scrapped on the site by Thos W. Ward. Andrew Barclay built the locomotive in 1954, works no. 2344, and it was supplied new to Clifton Colliery. After working a couple of stints at Babbington Colliery, the engine returned to Clifton before moving to Bestwood by March 1966. This was the only Andrew Barclay 0-6-0ST at the colliery.

Nottinghamshire, Bircotes, Harworth Colliery

Sinking of the colliery was completed by the end of 1923 and it was linked to the rail system by an LNER branch running west from Scrooby and one from the South Yorks Joint Railway. Standard-gauge railway usage came to an end in 1983. Built by Peckett & Sons in 1950, works no. 2110, this 0-4-0ST was delivered new to Welbeck Colliery and became Welbeck no. 8. By May 1959 it had moved to Harworth Colliery and became Harworth no. 2. A previous locomotive with this title was scrapped on site by August 1959. The second Harworth no. 2 was photographed in May 1971 and went to John Gretton, Market Overton, in April 1973. It is currently with the preservation site Rocks by Rail: the Living Ironstone Museum, near Oakham.

Nottinghamshire, Bulwell Forest, Rigley's Wagon Works

William Rigley established his company in 1896, building wagons and manufacturing mining machinery. The company's sidings were on the east side of the GNR Leen Valley line adjacent to Bulwell Forest railway station. Manning Wardle's 0-4-0ST *Stanlow*, works no. 1017, dating from 1887, was earlier at C. J. Willis & Sons Ltd, and was rebuilt in 1922. The engine had moved to Rigley's by 1927 and was photographed on 10 July 1949. It was scrapped on 17 November 1952. Rigley's Works closed on 31 December 1964.

Nottinghamshire, Cinderhill Colliery

The photograph was taken on 10 July 1949, three years before Babbington Colliery and Cinderhill Colliery officially became one, and renamed Babbington. The colliery was located west of Basford and Bulwell Station and rail traffic ceased around 1983. A merger with Hucknall Colliery occurred from January 1986, and the entire operation closed in October 1986. Robert Stephenson & Hawthorn's 0-6-0ST *Michael* dates from 1945, works no. 7285. The locomotive was ex-B. A. Collieries Ltd and went to W. Bagnall, Stratford, for repairs in 1956, before a return to Babbington. A little later the locomotive moved to Clifton Colliery and was scrapped by March 1966.

Nottinghamshire, Clifton Colliery

Clifton Nos '1 & 2' pits were originally owned by Clifton Colliery Company, Nottingham, and opened in 1871. The colliery was situated south-west of Arkwright Street railway station where it connected with several lines. After supplying coal for the nearby Wilford Power Station, and domestic fuel, closure came in July 1968. Hunslet's built 0-6-0ST *Philip*, works no. 2854, in 1943. The engine was ex-Bestwood Colliery and Babbington Colliery. Photographed in August 1967, it was scrapped by November 1969.

Nottinghamshire, Gedling Colliery

Gedling Colliery opened in 1899 and was formerly owned by Digby Colliery Co. Ltd. Closure came in 1991. The colliery was situated north-west of Gedling railway station and sidings stretched north-east from the BR line. Ruston & Hornsby's 0-4-0DM, works no. 375714, was built in 1955 and supplied new to Hucknall no. 2 Colliery (later Hucknall Colliery). The engine arrived at Gedling by July 1964 and was photographed on 12 May 1970. It was the only 0-4-0DM (no. 812478) at the colliery and went to C. F. Booth, Rotherham, on 28 November 1984.

Nottinghamshire, Gedling Colliery

Thomas Hill (Rotherham) Ltd built 4wDH *Susan*, works no. 176V, in 1966, and the loco was supplied new to Gedling Colliery. It was one of two 4wDH locomotives supplied by TH, the other one being *Gillian*, works no. 182V, in 1967. *Susan* was photographed on 12 May 1970 and both Gedling's 4wDH locomotives went to Booth Roe Metals Ltd, Rotherham, in August 1988.

Nottinghamshire, Gedling Colliery

Audrey was built by Peckett & Sons Ltd, works no. 1253, in 1911. The engine was delivered new and was one of two Pecketts at the colliery; the other one was also acquired new in 1903. Photographed on 30 January 1955, *Audrey* was scrapped on site by Nottingham Scrap Metal Co. Ltd by March 1969.

Nottinghamshire, Gedling Colliery
0-4-0ST *Queen*, built in 1923 by Andrew Barclay & Co., works no. 1784, was ex-Bromilow, Foster & Co. Ltd, Lancashire, and ex-Hough & Sons, Lancashire, before moving to Gedling in around 1932. The photograph was taken on 10 July 1949 and *Queen* was scrapped on site by Nottingham Scrap Metal Co. Ltd by March 1969.

Nottinghamshire, Gedling Colliery
Robert Stephenson & Hawthorns Ltd, Darlington Works, was responsible for building 0-6-0ST, works no. 6947, in 1938, becoming no. 39. The locomotive was ex-Appleby-Frodingham Steel Co. Ltd, Scunthorpe, moving to Gedling in April 1961. Photographed in 1966, the engine transferred to the Foxfield Railway, Dilhorne, Staffordshire, on 15 February 1970. It is currently located at the Darlington Railway Preservation Society, Darlington.

Nottinghamshire, Gedling Colliery

Hunslet's 0-6-0ST *King George* was erected in 1942, works no. 2409. The engine was ex-Linby Colliery, arriving at Gedling during February 1961. The photograph dates from 29 June 1970, and *King George* moved to Titanic Steamship Co. Ltd, Derbyshire, on 26 August 1977. The loco is presently with the Gloucester Warwickshire Steam Railway plc.

Nottinghamshire, Gedling Colliery

Andrew Barclay's 0-6-0ST *Catherine*, works no. 1000, was built in 1903 and supplied new to the colliery. Staying there throughout its working life, the engine was scrapped on the site by March 1966.

Nottinghamshire, Hucknall no. 2 Colliery

0-6-0ST *Sherwood no. 3* dates from 1899 when it was built by Manning Wardle, works no. 1440. The locomotive was ex-John Ellis & Son Ltd, Leicester (*Frank*), and moved to Sherwood Colliery in 1908. The engine then spent spells at Hucknall no. 1 Colliery, Hucknall no. 2 Colliery, Bestwood Colliery and Linby Colliery. Pictured here at Hucknall no. 2 Colliery on 10 July 1949, it was scrapped on site by July 1954.

Nottinghamshire, Kirkby Colliery (also known as Summit Colliery)

Formerly owned by the Butterley Co. Ltd, Kirkby Colliery was operational by 1890. It was situated between the Midland Railway's Mansfield to Kirkby line and the GNR's Leen Valley Extension line. Bagnall's 0-6-0ST *Butterley no. 30* was delivered new to the colliery in 1939, works no. 2604, at a cost of £2,260. The engine was photographed on 18 June 1955 and was sold or scrapped by May 1959. The colliery closed during July 1968.

Nottinghamshire, Kirkby Colliery (also known as Summit Colliery)
Lowca Engineering Co. Ltd, Cumbria, built 0-4-0ST *Pinxton* in 1907, works no. 246. The engine was delivered new, along with three other locos of the same class to Pinxton Collieries Ltd. The locomotive incorporated parts from Lowca Works nos 247 and 248 from 1950. *Pinxton* was photographed on 18 June 1955 before moving from Brookhill Colliery loco shed to Kirkby Colliery in August 1955. The loco was later transferred to Swanwick Colliery, Derbyshire, on 11 May 1958.

Nottinghamshire, Linby Colliery
Linby Colliery Co. Ltd sunk the pit between 1873 and 1875. The colliery, situated south from Linby railway station, was connected to both the ex LMSR and LNER lines running parallel past the site. Hunslet's built 0-6-0ST *Peter* in 1943, works no. 2853. Arriving at Linby by May 1964, the engine was ex-WD, France, Clifton Colliery, Hunslet, Bestwood Colliery, Babbington Colliery and Bestwood Central Workshops. Photographed in August 1967, *Peter* was scrapped on site during September 1972. The colliery closed in March 1988.

Nottinghamshire, Linby Colliery

Hudswell Clarke's 0-4-0ST, works no. 1797, was ordered by B. A. Collieries Ltd for Bestwood Colliery, but was delivered new to Hucknall no. 2 Colliery during April 1947. The engine, no. 8, moved to Linby by March 1966. The photograph, taken in August 1967, shows no. 8 in a dilapidated state; it was scrapped on site by March 1970.

Nottinghamshire, Mansfield Colliery (originally known as Crown Farm Colliery), Forest Town

Formerly owned by Bolsover Colliery Ltd, the colliery was sunk in 1904-05 and situated to the east of Mansfield railway station on the south side of the Mansfield GCR line. Hawthorne Leslie's 0-4-0ST *Diana* was delivered new to Thoresby Colliery, Edwinstowe, in 1937, works no. 3912. The engine moved to Mansfield in 1937. Photographed during February 1971, *Diana* was scrapped on site by March 1976.

Nottinghamshire, Moor Green Colliery, Eastwood
Barber, Walker & Co. Ltd played a large role in shaping Eastwood, owning the majority of the local pits. Thomas Barber was born at Greasley Castle Farm, and Thomas Walker at Bilborough. The company was formed in 1787, and remained active until nationalization in 1947. One of the company's pits, Moor Green, was sunk in 1868. Situated east of Eastwood and Langley Mill railway station, Moor Green Colliery was connected to both ex-LNER and ex-LMSR lines. The colliery closed in July 1985. Kitson's 0-6-0ST, works no. 1856, was built in 1873 and delivered new to Barber Walker & Co. The engine, no. 6, worked for a period at Harworth Colliery but was at Moor Green on Vesting Day 1 January 1947. No. 6 was photographed on 14 August 1954 and later went to Moor Green Central Workshops for scrap.

Nottinghamshire, Moor Green Colliery, Eastwood
This loco was ex-storage for the Ministry of Fuel & Power at Watnall by 27 July 1947, and ex-B Winning Colliery, Blackwell, Derbyshire, when it moved to Moor Green in October 1947. Built by Hunslet's in 1944, works no. 3196, it was photographed on 14 August 1954. The engine was transferred to Moor Green Central Workshops by May 1964 and then to Ashington Central Workshops, Nothumberland, by May 1965.

Nottinghamshire, New Hucknall Colliery

Sinking the New Hucknall Colliery at Huthwaite was completed by the late 1870s. It replaced Old Hucknall Colliery. The new colliery was situated south-west of Sutton-in-Ashfield and one of its first connections with the railway network was via a Midland Railway Co. branch line. Later, in 1893 it was connected via a branch to a MS&LR line running between Beighton and Annesley. The use of surface locomotives had ceased by 1980. Vulcan Foundry built 0-6-0ST no. 36 in 1945, works no. 5286. The engine was ex-Denby Hall Colliery, Derbyshire, and Moor Green Colliery and Moor Green Central Workshops, arriving at New Hucknall on 3 April 1969. Photographed during September 1971, no. 36 went to Nottingham Scrap Metal Co. Ltd, Basford, in January 1975.

Nottinghamshire, New Hucknall Colliery

Peckett's built 0-6-0ST *Swanwick Collieries no. 5* in 1940, works no.1972. The engine was ex-Swanwick Colliery, Derbyshire, before arriving at New Hucknall during 1961. The photograph dates from June 1970 and *Swanwick Collieries no. 5* went to Nottingham Scrap Metal Co. Ltd, Basford, on 13 November 1972.

Nottinghamshire, Newstead Colliery
Formerly owned by the Newstead Colliery Company and opening in 1874, the colliery was connected to ex-LMSR and ex-LNER lines running parallel past the site. Rail traffic ceased on 7 January 1984 and the colliery itself closed in March 1987. Hunslet's 0-4-0DH, works no. 5623, was built in 1960. The locomotive was hired initially, and then purchased by April 1962. On 30 January 1984, it was moved to Hucknall Colliery, acquiring the name *Ivor*, and then went C. F. Booth Ltd, Rotherham, on 30 October 1986.

Nottinghamshire, Newstead Colliery
During the 1920s, Sentinel developed a light shunting engine based on their steam lorries and tractors. An example is seen here in this 4w vertical boiler engine, *Windsor Castle*, works no. 9532, built in 1952. The vertical boiler is in the cab and the high-speed engine under the bonnet at the front. Between the cab and engine is the water tank. The loco was delivered new to Newstead along with *Glamis Castle* works no.9531. *Windsor Castle* moved to Kirkby Colliery by March 1963 and was scrapped by May 1966.

Nottinghamshire, Sherwood Colliery, Mansfield Woodhouse

The colliery dates from 1902 and was situated on the west side of the Midland Railway's line between Mansfield and Shirebrook. The use of standard-gauge locomotives ceased in 1983 and the colliery closed in 1992. Andrew Barclay built 0-6-0ST *Sherwood no. 1* in 1922, works no. 1638, and it was delivered new to the colliery. The engine replaced an earlier Manning Wardle locomotive of the same name that was moved to Thos W. Ward Ltd in around 1923. The photograph was taken on 10 September 1949 and *Sherwood no. 1* was scrapped by April 1967.

Nottinghamshire, Watnall

0-6-0T *Nancy* is pictured 'preserved' at C. F. & T. Stirland's premises, Watnall, in September 1971. The engine was built by Avonside Engineering in 1908, works no. 1547, and was delivered new to Brewers Grave Ironstone Quarries, Woolsthorpe. The locomotive also saw service at Harston Ironstone Quarries, Woolsthorpe, and Eastwell Ironstone Quarries before being transferred to Watnall in October 1961. Currently, *Nancy* is listed as being with Alan Keef Ltd, Ross-on-Wye, Hertfordshire.

Chapter 4

Oxfordshire to Worcestershire

Oxfordshire, Didcot Railway Centre
The Great Western Society was offered the use of the Didcot Motive Power Depot site and took
it over in 1967. The society has a comprehensive collection of ex-Great Western Railway (GWR)
locomotives and rolling stock. Robert Stephenson & Hawthorns built 0-4-0ST no. 1 *Bonnie Prince
Charlie*, works no.7544, in 1949. The engine was originally used by Messrs. Coral on Poole Quay.
Purchased for preservation by the Salisbury Steam Trust in 1969, *Bonnie Prince Charlie* moved to
Didcot shortly afterwards. The locomotive was photographed in October 1969.

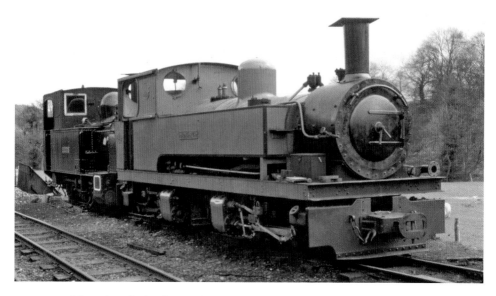

Powys, Welshpool and Llanfair Light Railway
The Welshpool and Llanfair Light Railway (W&LLR) is a narrow-gauge – 2-ft-6-in. – heritage railway in Powys, Wales, and was opened in 1963. Because of the gauge, unusual for the UK, some locomotives and rolling stock were obtained from a cosmopolitan variety of sources. *Monarch*, an articulated Bagnall-Meyer 0-4-4-0T, seen here in April 1977, was the last narrow-gauge steam loco built for British industry and it went to the Bowaters' Paper Railway in Kent. The engine was built in 1953 and its name commemorates the Coronation of that year. In 1966 *Monarch* was sold to the Welshpool & Llanfair Light Railway, but was not initially a success; in 1992, it was acquired for the Ffestiniog Railway. However, ten years later, *Monarch* was re-purchased by the W&LLR.

Powys, Welshpool and Llanfair Light Railway
Kerr Stuart's 0-6-2T *Joan*, works no. 4401, dates from 1929 and originally operated in Antigua. The locomotive arrived at Llanfair in 1971.

Rutland, Rutland Railway Museum, Cottesmore
The museum's website states proudly: 'Our Museum sets out to preserve and recreate the essential elements of a typical East Midlands ironstone quarrying operation as it may have been seen in its heyday during the 1950's or 1960's but with some additional artefacts and exhibits.' Hunslet, works no. 2868 of 1943, rebuilt (3883) in 1963, was pictured there in December 1980. It was purchased from the Rutland Railway Museum by Peak Rail in 2008 and has become known as *Lord Phil*. Earlier details of the locomotive are given in the Glasshoughton colliery section where the locomotive is seen at work.

Stafford, Stafford Railway Station
0-4-0ST *Isabel* was built in 1897 by W. Bagnall, works no. 1491, for the 2-ft-gauge Cliffe Hill Quarry Railway in Leicestershire. The engine was sold back to Bagnall's in 1952, and it is shown here on a plinth in front of Stafford railway station. It is now preserved at the Amerton Railway, a 2-ft-narrow-gauge heritage railway in Staffordshire. The photograph was taken in May 1971.

Opposite above: Staffordshire, Bass, Ratcliffe & Gretton Ltd, Burton-on-Trent
Bass was founded in 1777 and the company acquired its first locomotive in 1863. Throughout the remainder of the century, as the size of the company's operation increased, a large locomotive fleet was established to operate a system of private lines. They also connected to a number of Midland Railway branches throughout the town, with rail traffic finally coming to a halt in May 1967. *No. 7* was built by Thornewill & Wareham as a 0-4-0 well tank, works no. 400, in 1875 and supplied new to Bass. The engine was rebuilt in 1899 as a saddle tank locomotive by Hunslet. *No. 7* went to Thos. W. Ward, Sheffield, for scrap in March 1963.

Opposite below: Staffordshire, Bass, Ratcliffe & Gretton Ltd, Burton-on-Trent
Bass, Ratcliffe & Gretton Ltd operated no. fewer than twelve locomotives similar to the design of the engine illustrated. 0-4-0 no. 2 was built by Neilson Reid & Co. in 1900, works no. 5760. The locomotive went to Thos. W. Ward, Friargate Goods Yard, Derby, for scrap in August 1964.

Above: Staffordshire, Cannock Wood Colliery
The Cannock & Rugeley Colliery Co. Ltd sunk the colliery in 1866. It was connected to the Cannock Chase Railway, built for the LNWR in 1863 to serve the brickworks and collieries within the area. Cannock Wood Colliery's 0-6-0ST no. 7 *Wimblebury*, was built by Hunslet, works no. 3839, and supplied new to Rawnsley Shed in 1956. In 1963/64 the engine spent time at Cannock Central Workshops before a return to Cannock Wood Colliery. Photographed on 17 May 1971, *Wimblebury* moved to Foxfield RPS during September 1973.

Staffordshire, Chasewater Light Railway and Museum Co. Ltd

Beginning as the Railway Preservation Society, the organisation existed until 1972 when it became the Chasewater Light Railway changing to Chasewater Light Railway and Museum Co. Ltd in 1987. In 1966 the Society acquired a section of track from the NCB which was part of the Cannock Chase Colliery system. It also included a short stretch which had extended to Conduit Colliery. The railway is home to a one of the premier collections of industrial steam and diesel locomotives, many with local connections. R & W Hawthorne Leslie's 0-4-0ST *Asbestos*, built in 1909, works no. 2780, was presented to the society by Turner's Asbestos Cement Co. Ltd, Trafford Park, Manchester, on 15 June 1968.

Staffordshire, Foxfield Light Railway, Dilhorne

The Foxfield Light Railway is a preserved standard-gauge line located south-east of Stoke-on-Trent. It was constructed in 1893 to serve the colliery at Dilhorne on the Cheadle Coalfield. 0-4-0ST no. 3, works no. 3581, was presented to the FLR on 12 April 1967. The loco was supplied new by Hawthorne Leslie to Burton-on-Trent brewers, Marston Thompson & Evershed Ltd, in 1924. The engine was photographed in May 1971.

Staffordshire, Foxfield Light Railway, Dilhorne

Bagnall built 0-4-0ST *J. T. Daly* in 1931, works no. 2450. It moved to Foxfield from Horsley Bridge & Thomas Piggott Ltd in Dudley Port, West Midlands, in July 1969. Photographed in September 1970, the loco was sold for use on the Alderney Railway in the Channel Islands, and left in August 1982. After several years of use on Alderney hauling London Underground rolling stock, it is now with the Steam Motor & General Museum, Jersey.

Staffordshire Littleton Colliery, Huntington

Sinking operations at the colliery were completed in 1889. Initially, the colliery was connected to the rail network via a branch to the LNRW's Wolverhampton to Stafford line. There was also a line to sidings at the canal side at Otherton. Rationalisation of the colliery's rail traffic occurred in around 1977, following the installation of a rapid loading bunker. Littleton Colliery closed in 1993 and was the last deep mine in Staffordshire. Built by the Yorkshire Engine Co. in 1959, works no. 2748, 0-6-0DE *no. 6* was supplied new to Hilton Main Colliery. The engine moved to Littleton on 8 July 1966 and was photographed on 17 May 1971. *No. 6* was transferred to Peak Rail, Buxton on 14 July 1988 but is currently with Churnet Valley Railway.

Above and below: Staffordshire Littleton Colliery, Huntington

Manning Wardle supplied 0-6-0ST *Littleton no. 5*, works no. 2018, new to the colliery in 1922, and it spent all its working life there. Prior to Vesting Day, 1 January 1947, the colliery operated seven Manning Wardle locomotives; four of these were supplied new. The top photograph was taken on 17 May 1971, the one below in June of the same year. The engine was moved to Foxfield RPS during October 1972, but has since relocated to the Avon Valley Railway Co. Ltd.

Staffordshire Littleton Colliery, Huntington

Hudswell Clarke built 0-6-0ST *no.* 7, works no. 1752, in 1943. The engine was ex-WD 75091 before a move to Holly Bank loco Shed in October 1950. A transfer to Littleton Colliery occurred on 12 January 1959 where the engine was photographed on 7 June 1971. *No.* 7 was transferred to Bold Colliery, Lancashire on 27 February 1978, but is now with the Great Central Railway plc, Loughborough.

Staffordshire, Littleton Colliery, Huntington

0-6-0ST *Robert Nelson no. 4* was supplied new, works no. 1800, to Holly Bank Colliery by Hunslet in 1936. The loco moved to Littleton Colliery on 10 January 1959. Photographed in June 1971, it went to Foxfield RPS, Dilhorne, north Staffordshire, in October 1972. The Riverstown Mill Railway, near Dundalk, presently holds the locomotive.

Staffordshire, West Cannock No. 5 Colliery, Hednesford

West Cannock no. 5 Colliery was owned by the West Cannock Colliery Company Ltd. Both shafts were sunk for no. 5 by 1916. The colliery and sidings were situated north of Hednesford railway station. The end for rail traffic came in December 1977 and the colliery itself closed in December 1982. 0-6-0ST *Topham* was supplied new, works no. 2193, to Brindley Heath Colliery or West Cannock no. 5 Colliery by W. Bagnall in 1922. The engine spent time at West Cannock no. 1-3 Colliery, Cannock Central Workshops and Cannock Wood Colliery, and was photographed on 17 May 1971. During October 1972 *Topham* moved to Foxfield RPS, but it is currently located at Tunbridge Wells & Eridge Railway Preservation Society Ltd, Tunbridge Wells.

Staffordshire, West Cannock No. 5 Colliery, Hednesford

Hunslet built 'Austerity' 0-6-0ST no. 4 and it was supplied new to Rawnsley Shed (one of two 0-6-0STs) in 1953, works no. 3806. The engine was ex-Cannock Chase Loco Shed before a move to West Cannock no. 5 in August 1957, where it spent the rest of its working life. No. 4 was photographed on 17 May 1971 and went to Dean Forest RPS, Gloucestershire, around March 1973, where it has acquired the name 'Wilbert' after the Revd Wilbert Awdry.

Sussex, Bluebell Railway Co. Ltd

The Bluebell Railway is a heritage line running for 9 miles along the border between East and West Sussex. Steam-hauled trains are operated between Sheffield Park and Kingscote, with an intermediate station at Horsted Keynes. The railway is managed and run largely by volunteers and has a collection of over thirty steam locomotives. No. 3 *Captain Baxter* arrived at the Bluebell in 1960 after spending its working life at the Dorking Greystone Lime Works at Betchworth Station. The 0-4-0T, built in 1877 by Fletcher Jennings, works no. 158, was photographed in August 1969 and returned to traffic in 1982 after a comprehensive overhaul. Further work was carried out in 2010 and the engine returned to steam at Bluebell's 50th Anniversary celebrations in August 2010.

Swansea, Brynlliw Colliery

The original Brynlliw Colliery at Grovesend, 2 miles south-east of Pontardulais, closed in pre-NCB days. But in the mid-1950s the NCB reconstructed and reopened it, and it remained in production until 1983. The picture shows an unidentified 'Austerity' 0-6-0ST at the colliery in April 1976.

Worcestershire/Shropshire, Severn Valley Railway

The Severn Valley Railway is a heritage railway in Shropshire and Worcestershire. The 16-mile line runs along the Severn Valley from Bridgnorth to Kidderminster, crossing the Shropshire/ Worcestershire border, following the course of the River Severn for much of its route. Hunslet 0-6-0T no. 686 of 1898 was a shunting engine *no. 14 St. John* on the Manchester Ship Canal railway system. It was displaced by diesels on the MSC in 1958 when it was sold to ICI for use at their Blackley dyestuffs works. It was renamed *Lady Armaghdale* at that time. The Blackley rail system was closed in December 1968, and the following year the loco was sold for preservation. Photographed in November 1971, the loco became *Thomas the Tank Engine* in 1994, and performed at steam heritage lines throughout the UK before retiring in 2009.

Worcestershire/Shropshire, Severn Valley Railway

Manning Wardle's 0-6-0ST *Warwickshire*, works no. 2047, was built in 1926. For thirteen years the engine was on static display at Kidderminster Railway Museum, but it returned in 2010 to the Severn Valley Railway to be dismantled and assessed for a possible return to working order. The photograph was taken in April 1972.

Chapter 5
Yorkshire

Yorkshire, Acton Hall Colliery

Sinking began at Acton Hall Colliery in 1877. It was situated on the north side of the Lancashire & Yorkshire Railway's Wakefield to Goole line. The colliery and its brickworks were connected to this line and also to the east end of the Midland Railway's Snydale branch. A number of working locomotives were kept at Featherston Main Colliery (closed 1935) loco shed until 1962. Acton Hall also supplied locomotives to work traffic from Snydale Colliery Washery until around 1965. In *Railway Bylines* (January 2000) it is mentioned that when BR used Class 47 diesels on the merry-go-round trains from Acton Hall exchange sidings, these locomotives sometimes struggled to get away from the sidings and up the gradient past the colliery. Therefore it was not unknown for one of the colliery locomotives to go out to the main line and bank the BR train. At least three of the Acton Hall engines were authorised to run on BR metals. *Airedale* was built in 1923 by Hunslet's, works no. 1440. The engine was the first Standard 15 in Hunslet design, and so the class was also known as the 'Airedale' class. The official delivery date to Airedale Collieries Ltd was 23 July 1923. The locomotive spent time at Peckfield Colliery, Newmarket Colliery, Allerton Bywater Central Workshops and West Riding Colliery, before transfer to Acton Hall in January 1963. The colliery closed in July 1985. *Airedale* arrived for preservation at Embsay on 22 December 1975. Two other Acton Hall locos are also present at Embsay: *Beatrice* and S112, while Acton Hall no. 3 went to Worth Valley Railway.

Above and below: Yorkshire, Acton Hall Colliery
Bagnall 'Austerity' 0-6-0ST, NCB 143, was built in 1944, works no. 2740. It was ex-WD, Long
Marston, Warwickshire, arriving at Acton Hall via Allerton Bywater Central Workshops in 1966.
The top photograph was taken on 16 September 1971; the one below, 23 August 1971. The loco
was scrapped on site by Wakefield Metal Traders Ltd in July 1976.

Yorkshire, Darfield Colliery

Formerly owned by Mitchell Main Colliery Ltd, two shafts were sunk at Darfield in 1860, a third one being added later. The colliery was served by sidings running north from the BR line, half a mile north-west of Wombwell railway station. Standard-gauge locomotive usage had stopped by 1982, and the colliery was merged with Houghton Main in November 1986, finally closing three years later. *Darfield no. 1*, a Hunslet 0-6-0ST, was supplied new in 1953, works no. 3783. The engine was at Houghton Main Colliery from 1955-59, and was photographed on 5 April 1971. It went to A. Hall, Delph, Oldham, in 1974, but moved to Embsay in December 1975.

Yorkshire, Dodworth Colliery

Dodworth Colliery was originally owned by Old Silkstone Collieries and known as Church Lane Pit. It became Old Silkstone Colliery and later Dodworth, shafts 2 and 3 being sunk in 1850. The Redbrook shaft was sunk nearby in 1903. After 1947, there was also a satellite unit at Higham, a mile to the north. Sidings served Dodworth Colliery and extended north from the BR (ex-LNER) line, north-east of Dodworth railway station. Dodworth and Higham were linked by overland conveyor, but the latter had no rail connection. The above 0-6-0ST was built at Hunslet in 1943, works no. 2857, and became ex-WD. Photographed on 6 August 1971, it later went to Cadley Hill, Derbyshire.

Yorkshire, Dodworth Colliery
NCB 0-6-0ST no. 1 was erected by Hudswell Clarke in 1960, works no. 1889, and was supplied new to Monk Bretton Colliery, arriving at Dodworth during October 1968. Photographed on 6 August 1971, it was scrapped on site in March 1975.

Yorkshire, Embsay and Bolton Abbey Steam Railway
The Embsay & Bolton Abbey Steam Railway (E&BASR) is a heritage railway in North Yorkshire (formed in 1968 and reopened in 1979). The rolling stock on the line includes approximately twenty ex-industrial locomotives. The Yorkshire Engine Company built 0-4-0ST 4-ft-8½-in.-gauge *York no. 1* in 1949, works no. 2474. It was formerly based at Wombwell Colliery, Birdwell Central Workshops, Barnsley Main Colliery, Monk Bretton Colliery, Wharncliffe Woodmoor nos 4 & 5 Colliery and South Kirby Colliery until 19 September 1975, when it was transferred to Embsay. The Embsay website states this is a very rare locomotive as only two other YE Co. engines exist in preservation, both 0-6-0STs.

Yorkshire, Embsay and Bolton Abbey Steam Railway
Avonside no. 1908, 0-4-0ST *Fred*, was originally with ICI at Northwich. Later the engine was bought by Doncaster enthusiast Terry Robinson and kept in Doncaster MPD for a while. Then it went to Carcoft Station, Doncaster, for restoration. *Fred* later moved to Market Overton, Embsay (seen here in June 1972), and the Nene Valley Railway from 1976-81. *Fred* was eventually sold to the present owner in Maldegem, Belgium.

Yorkshire, Embsay and Bolton Abbey Steam Railway
Sentinel 0-4-0VBT *Ann* was built in 1927, works no. 7232. The locomotive spent its entire working life at British Tar at Irlam, Manchester, until withdrawal around 1969. It was photographed at the Embsay & Bolton Abbey Steam Railway in June 1972. A restoration programme was undertaken by Ian Douglas, Embsay's treasurer, in 1995, and the locomotive returned to steam in early 1998. Embsay's 2004 Harvest of Steam saw *Ann* operating once more and hauling, for the first time in its history, a passenger train. Because the loco is not fitted with a vacuum brake, a visiting Peckett provided the vacuum, and *Ann's* crew had a brake valve in the cab.

Yorkshire, Embsay and Bolton Abbey Steam Railway
No. 22, 0-4-0ST *East Hetton Colliery*, was erected by Andrew Barclay in 1952, works no. 2320. The red livery, carried when at work at East Hetton, was the one adopted for most of its time on the railway. The Embsay website states that no. 22 was originally no. 53, and was new to East Hetton Colliery. From there it went to several other collieries on loan for various periods. Its last transfer was to Fishburn Coking Plant in 1974. The website also adds: 'Basically the engine is rough riding, a poor steamer and now with a 5 mile run, the railway soon outstrips its coal capacity. What has never been in doubt is its power.'

Yorkshire, Emley Moor colliery, Huddersfield

Initially owned by Stringer & Jagger Ltd (later Stringer & Son) Emley Moor pit was in production by the 1850s. The screening plant was served by sidings which ran north from the BR line adjacent to Skelmanthorpe railway station. Rail traffic ceased at the colliery in July 1982 and the colliery itself closed in 1985. 0-4-0ST, NCB No. 3, *Standback*, was built by Hudswell Clarke in 1953, works no. 1817. The locomotive was supplied new to Hartley Bank colliery, arriving at Emley Moor in February 1968. *Standback* is seen here on 6 August 1971. It was scrapped on site by Roe Brothers & Co. Rotherham during August 1976.

Yorkshire, Fryston Colliery

Fryston Colliery opened in the 1870s and closed in December 1985. The colliery's sidings were 2½ miles east of Castleford railway station and north of the BR (ex-LNER) line. An NCB line connected Fryston to Wheldale Colliery, while other lines gave access to tips and staiths. During both Fryston and Wheldale's existence, locomotives normally allocated to one colliery could sometimes be seen at the other. The use of predominantly Hunslet 0-6-0ST locos during NCB years was a feature at Fryston. But NCB 0-6-0T *Fryston no. 2*, one of two Hudswell Clarke locos at the colliery, was supplied new in 1955, works no. 1883. A mechanical stoker was fitted to the loco by Hunslet in 1963/64. *No. 2* was photographed at Fryston on 16 September 1971, and was scrapped on site by Wakefield Metal Traders Ltd in September 1972.

Opposite above: Yorkshire, Fryston Colliery

NCB no. 1, *Rose Louise,* a Hudswell Clarke 0-6-0DM, was built in 1956, works no. D972, and supplied new to Whitwood Colliery, moving to Fryston in November 1968. It was the only 0-6-0 DM noted at the colliery in NCB days. Photographed in May 1972, *Rose Louise* was scrapped on site by C. F. Booth of Rotherham in July 1985. Fryston's three remaining diesels – two 0-6-0DH locomotives and a single 0-4-0DH – were transferred to Wheldale Colliery in 1986.

Opposite below: Yorkshire, Glasshoughton Colliery

Deep mining began at Glasshoughton in 1869. There was also a coking plant at the colliery and both were linked by rail. Colliery and coking plant sidings were situated south-east of Castleford Cutsyke railway station. Surface locomotives ceased to be used from 1973. The coking plant closed in 1978 and the colliery in March 1986. NCB 0-6-0ST *Coal Products no. 6* was built by Hunslet in 1943, works no. 2868. The locomotive was ex-MoD Shoeburyness and worked at Glasshoughton Coking Plant. It was also rebuilt by Hunslet during the early 1960s and fitted with a mechanical stoker, moving to BR Western region for test runs before arrival at Glasshoughton Colliery in February1971. The loco was photographed on 16 September 1971, and was transferred to Market Overton Industrial Railway Association on 29 March 1979.

Opposite above: Yorkshire, Glasshoughton Colliery
Hunslet supplied 0-6-0T S118 new to Glasshoughton Colliery in 1953, works no. 1870. The locomotive spent time at Ackton Hall Colliery, Glasshoughton Coking Plant, and was also fitted with a mechanical stoker. The engine was one of two 0-6-0Ts working at Glasshoughton in the NCB period. Seen here in May 1972, it was scrapped on site by Wakefield Metal Traders Ltd, during April 1973.

Opposite below: Yorkshire, Grimethorpe Colliery
The first sod was cut for the new Grimethorpe Colliery in October 1894 and operations conducted by the Mitchell Main Colliery Co. yielded the first coal in 1897. The colliery and sidings were connected to the rail system via a branch to a former LMSR line and one to the Dearne Valley line. BR made a new connection, replacing these older lines in the 1950s. Standard-gauge locomotive operation had ceased by 1986 and the colliery closed in May 1993. Vulcan Foundry erected 0-6-0ST no. 4 in 1945, works no. 5295. The engine, ex-Carlton Main Colliery, went to Hunslet 1965/66 and was photographed on 5 April 1971. In June 1972 it was scrapped on site by Thos. W. Ward Ltd.

Above: Yorkshire, Grimethorpe Colliery
Hudswell Clarke's 0-4-0DM, works no. D1094, built in 1959, was delivered new to Shafton Central Workshops, Shafton, and moved to Grimethorpe in January 1971. Photographed in April 1971, it went to Park Mill Colliery, West Yorkshire, in October 1972. In 1981, the loco departed for Gascoigne Wood Colliery, North Yorks, but its presence there has not been confirmed.

Yorkshire, Keighley & Worth Valley, Haworth

The Keighley & Worth Valley Railway is a 5-mile-long heritage branch line, operated in its original form, in West Yorkshire. It runs from Keighley to Oxenhope, connecting to the national rail network line at Keighley railway station. Hudswell Clarke's 0-6-0T no. 31 *Hamburg* was built in 1903, works no. 679, and formerly worked at the Manchester Ship Canal Railway. The standard-gauge railway was built to service freight to and from the canal's docks and nearby industrial estates, and connected to the various railway companies that had track near the canal. At its peak, the MSCL had approximately seventy-five locomotives. *Hamburg* is pictured in preservation at Haworth in April 1972.

Yorkshire, Keighley & Worth Valley, Haworth

Manning Wardle 0-6-0ST *Sir Berkeley* was built in 1891, works no. 1210, and was supplied new to Logan & Hemingway, a firm of engineering contractors. In 1935 L&H went into liquidation and the engine was sold to the Cranford Ironstone Company of Kettering, Northamptonshire, where it received the nameplates *Sir Berkeley* from a scrapped Manning Wardle engine. It was bought in 1964 by Roger Crombleholme, and eventually taken to the Worth Valley Railway. The locomotive appeared in the 1968 BBC TV version of *The Railway Children*. Photographed at Haworth in August 1968, *Sir Berkeley* has travelled extensively within this country and abroad. The Middleton Railway at Leeds is its present location.

Yorkshire, Markham Main Colliery, Armthorpe

Markham Main Colliery opened in the mid-1920s. It was connected to the rail network via a branch from the old South Yorkshire Joint line. Standard-gauge locomotives were not used after 1989. Final closure at the colliery came in 1996. Hunslet's built 0-6-0ST *Arthur*, works no. 3782, in 1952, and it was delivered new to the colliery. The engine went to Titanic Salvage Co. Ltd, Ellastone, Staffordshire, on 21 January 1977. The Quainton Railway Society, Buckinghamshire, website adds further details: '*Arthur* was out of use until 1978, when it was moved to Crab Key, Ellastone, near Ashbourne, Derbyshire, where it joined a private collection of industrial engines. A year later it was moved to High Cogges near Witney, Oxfordshire, but arrived at Quainton on 1st December 1979.'

Yorkshire, Middleton Railway

The Middleton Railway, Leeds is the oldest commercially successful railway in the world, beginning life back in 1758 when it was the first railway constructed by order of an Act of Parliament. Built originally to carry coal from the vast Middleton pits, the railway was also the first standard gauge to come under preservation back in 1960. It is now run by volunteers from the Middleton Railway Trust Ltd. One of Middleton's locomotives, Hudswell Clarke 0-4-0ST *Henry De Lacy II*, built in 1917, works no. 1309, worked in Kirkstall Forge, Leeds, from delivery until closure of the works' railway system in 1968. The engine went to the MRT in February 1969 and the photograph was taken in October of that year.

Yorkshire, Newmarket Colliery, Stanley
Newmarket was sunk in 1837 and the original owners were the Fenton Brothers, later J. & J. Charlesworths. The colliery and sidings were located a mile to the east of Stanley railway station. Lines also ran to a staith at Cringleworth, spoil heaps and a junction at Royds Green Lower. Rail traffic ceased in 1981 and the colliery closed two years later. 0-6-0ST *Jubilee* was built by Hunslet in 1935, works no.1726, and was ex-Waterloo Main Colliery before arriving at Newmarket in January 1966. Pictured on 16 September 1971, *Jubilee* was scrapped on site by Wakefield Metal Traders Ltd in March 1973.

Opposite above: Yorkshire, Newmarket Colliery, Stanley
Hudswell Clarke built 0-6-0DM, NCB no. 16, in 1960, works no. D1137 – one of two DMs delivered new to Newmarket Colliery in that year. The colliery had a total of five DMs and two DHs in nationalisation years. Photographed on 16 September 1971, no. 16 was scrapped on site by R. E. Trem Ltd of Finningley, Doncaster, in February 1977.

Opposite below: Yorkshire, Newmarket Colliery, Stanley
Ex-Waterloo Main Colliery's 0-6-0ST *Jess*, built by Hunslet in 1943, works no. 2876, arrived at Newmarket in November 1968. Whilst at Waterloo the engine returned to Hunslet in September 1961 and was fitted with a prototype mechanical stoker. V. J. Bradley (2002) also records that it returned there on a number of occasions for 'modification and adjustment.' Photographed on 16 September 1971, *Jess* was scrapped on site by W. H. Arnott, Young & Co. Ltd of Bradford in November 1973.

Yorkshire, North Gawber Colliery

The colliery was sunk during the early 1850s when development was encouraged by the Lancashire & Yorkshire Railway branch line linking Horbury and Barnsley at the beginning of the decade. The colliery was linked to the railway network via a branch line which extended westwards from the ex-L& Y line, south-east of Darton railway station. From 1948, coal from Darton Colliery was wound from North Gawber. Pictured in a sorry state on 6 August 1971, 0-6-0ST no. 61 was built by Hunslet in 1945, works no. 3212. The engine was ex-WD, Shoeburyness, Essex, before moving to North Gawber in April 1964. It was scrapped on site by Walter Heselwood Ltd in April 1977.

Yorkshire, North Gawber Colliery

Hudswell Clarke supplied 0-6-0T, works no. 1857, new to North Gawber in 1952. It arrived at the colliery painted green but was later repainted maroon. Photographed on 6 August 1971, the loco went to Shackerstone Railway Society, Leicester, on 6 August 1975. Later, there was a move to the Swindon & Cricklade Railway, but the engine has since relocated to Henstridge in Somerset.

Yorkshire, North Gawber Colliery

In January 1986, North Gawber merged with Woolley Colliery and the surface facilities and colliery closed at the same time. Barclay's 0-4-0ST, built in 1945, works no. 2195, was ex-Workington Iron & Steel Co. Ltd, Cumberland and Hartley Bank Colliery, before arriving at North Gawber in June 1968. In *Railway Bylines Vol. 14* (January 2009), Steven Oakden says the intention of the transfer from Hartley Bank is unclear, 'but whatever [the reason], the loco was considered too small and was never used.' Photographed on 6 August 1971, the engine was scrapped on site by Walter Haselwood Ltd, during June 1972.

Yorkshire, North Yorkshire Moors Railway, Goathland

First opened in 1836 as the Whitby & Pickering Railway, the railway was planned in 1831 by George Stephenson as a means of opening up trade routes inland from the then important seaport of Whitby. The line closed in 1965 but was reopened in 1973 by the North York Moors Historical Railway Trust Ltd. The preserved line is now a significant tourist attraction and has been awarded many industry accolades. 0-4-0ST *Mirvale*, built by Hudswell Clarke in 1955, works no. 1882, worked at the Mirvale Chemical Co. of Mirfield until 1964. Four years later the engine entered preservation at the North York Moors Railway. It soon proved too small for their requirements and went to the Middleton Railway in 1986. *Mirvale* was photographed at Goathland in September 1971.

Yorkshire, Peckfield colliery, Mickelfield

Peckfield Colliery, once owned by Joseph Cliff & Sons, was in production by the 1870s. The Peckfield Colliery sidings were half a mile west of Mickelfield railway station on the south side of the BR (ex-LNER) line. The colliery closed in October 1986. 0-6-0T S100 *Whitwood no. 1* was built by Hudswell Clarke in 1949, works no. 1822. The engine was delivered new to Whitwood Colliery and later moved to Water Haigh Colliery, Prince of Wales Colliery and Allerton Bywater Central Workshops, before arriving at Peckfield in May 1961. It went to Hunslet for repairs and to be fitted with a mechanical stoker in 1964/65. A stint at Allerton Bywater Central Workshops followed in 1968/69, before a return once more to Peckfield. Photographed on 23 August1971, the loco went to the Yorkshire Dales Railway, Embsay, on 23 July 1973. It is currently at Chasewater.

Yorkshire, Peckfield Colliery, Mickelfield

NCB 0-6-0DM no. 3 was one of two DMs at Peckfield Colliery during the nationalisation period. Built by Hudswell Clarke in 1957, works no. D974, the loco was delivered new to Whitwood Colliery, arriving at Peckfield in April 1968. Photographed on 23 August 1971, it was scrapped on site by Wakefield Metal Traders Ltd by August 1976.

Yorkshire, Peckfield Colliery, Mickelfield

NCB S.121 0-6-0ST *Primrose no.2* was erected by Hunslet to their standard 16-in. design in 1952, works no. 3715. The engine was delivered new to Primrose Colliery and returned to Hunslet for repairs and the fitting of a mechanical stoker in 1963/64. Having gone back to Primrose Colliery, it arrived, ex-Allerton Bywater Central Workshops, at Peckfield in September 1971. Photographed in April 1972, *Primrose no. 2* was transferred to the Yorkshire Dales Railway, Embsay, in December 1973, where in past years it has been one of the main engines for the railway.

Yorkshire, Prince of Wales Colliery

The Prince of Wales Colliery was in production by the mid-1870s and was connected to the main line railway network immediately west of Pontefract railway station. Between 1877 and the 1890s, one locomotive – an 0-4-0ST – was in sole charge of internal shunting. Thereafter a further five locomotives were acquired and these lasted until the 1950s. In *Railway Bylines Vol. 4 no. 10*, Adrian Booth states that the colliery's railway sidings – which could accommodate some 1,000 wagons – were a hive of activity, adding: 'The "main line" locomotive brought in empty wagons, which the colliery's own shunting engine divided up into smaller rakes and moved into the "empties" sidings.' Vulcan Foundry built 0-6-0ST, works no. 5276, in 1945. The engine was ex-WD Shoeburyness and Allerton Bywater Central Workshops before moving to Prince of Wales Colliery around July 1965. Photographed in August 1971, the engine was scrapped on site in November 1972.

Yorkshire, Prince of Wales Colliery

Hudswell Clarke's 0-6-0T, built in 1956, works no. 1886, moved from Whitwood Colliery (no. 8) to Prince of Wales in around 1958. It was painted in a livery of maroon and black with yellow lettering on the tank sides. Photographed on 23 August 1971, the engine was scrapped on the site in December 1972. Adrian Booth (*op. cit.*) states that steam locomotives were available for operation at Prince of Wales '– in theory at least – until the mid 1970s.' Prince of Wales closed in December 1980, but men were transferred to the drift mine of the same name which was opened earlier in that year. Around that time the colliery was converted for merry-go-round operation, and the surface standard-gauge railway and screens were taken out of use around July 1979. The Prince of Wales drift mine closed in 2002.

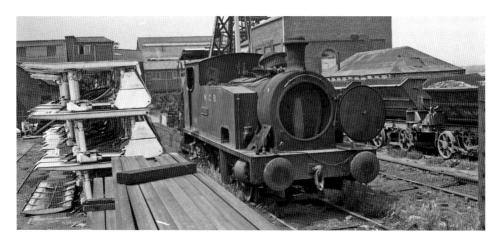

Yorkshire, Savile Colliery, Mickletown, near Methley

Savile Colliery was formerly owned by H. Briggs Son & Co. Ltd/Briggs Collieries until 1 July 1939. It opened around 1876 and there was a rail connection via a line which ran east from BR (ex-LMSR) north of Methley Station. Lines also ran to a staith on the Aire & Calder navigation to the north of the colliery, and a tip to the east. Savile was placed in the NCB North Eastern Division, area no. 8 from 1 January 1947. In around 1965, rail traffic ceased to and from BR, and internal traffic followed in 1982. The colliery closed three years later. NCB 0-6-0T, S112, *Elizabeth*, was built by Hudswell Clarke in 1927, works no. 1600. The engine was formerly at Allerton Bywater Central Workshops and Water Haigh Colliery before being scrapped at Savile in November 1971, the year this photograph was taken.

Yorkshire, Savile Colliery, Mickletown, near Methley
Hudswell Clarke 0-6-0DM, NCB no. 5, was built in 1958, works no. D1070. The locomotive arrived new at Wheldale Colliery, moving to Savile by February 1968. It was disused by 11 June 1983 and scrapped on the site by C. F. Booth Ltd in September 1985. The photograph dates from September 1971.

Yorkshire, Savile Colliery, Mickletown, near Methley
Hunslet was responsible for building 0-6-0ST *Airedale no. 2* in 1939, works no. 1956. The locomotive had spells at Airedale Collieries Ltd, Fryston Colliery and Wheldale Colliery, before moving to Savile in 1962. Hunslet fitted a mechanical stoker to the locomotive in 1964. Pictured at Saville on 16 September 1971, *Airedale no. 2* was scrapped by Wakefield Metal Traders Ltd in November 1975.

Yorkshire Skiers Spring Colliery, Wentworth (part of Rockingham Colliery)
A drift mine established at the site of Skiers Spring (Wentworth North) Disposal Point handled part of the output of Rockingham Colliery between 1952 and 1975. It replaced the Wentworth Disposal Point (also known as Harley Stocking Ground) existing between 1942 and 1947 on the former exchange sidings of the closed Lidget Colliery. NCB 0-4-0ST no. 4 was built by Hudswell Clarke, works no. 1892, in 1961. It arrived new at Barnsley Main then went to Wombwell Colliery and moved to Skiers Spring in November 1969. Photographed on 6 August 1971, it was taken to Titanic Salvage Co. Ltd, Ellastone, Staffordshire, on 29 January 1977.

Yorkshire Skiers Spring Colliery, Wentworth (part of Rockingham Colliery)
Hudswell Clarke supplied 0-4-0ST NCB, no. 3, new to Skiers Spring in 1961, works no. 1891. The loco was one of two Hudswell Clarke locos that arrived at the colliery during nationalisation. No. 3 is pictured on 6 August 1971 and was scrapped on site by Ogden Ltd in May 1975.

Yorkshire, South Kirkby

Sinking operations in the South Kirkby area were begun by the Ferryhill & Rosedale Iron Company reaching the Barnsley seam in August 1878. Disappointingly, the owners ran out of cash, but a new limited company, with John Shaw of Darrington Hall as chairman, took over in 1880, and work progressed apace. Under nationalisation, there were two connections to the BR network: one north-west of South Elmsall railway station, and another at the south end of the colliery area. The use of surface locomotives ceased around September 1970. The colliery itself closed in March 1988. NCB no.1, *John Shaw*, presumably named after the former colliery owner, was built by Hunslet in 1942, works no. 2375. Photographed on 5 April 1971, the engine was scrapped on site by Thos W. Ward Ltd, Sheffield, in January 1972. To the rear is 0-4-0ST *York no. 1*, whose details are mentioned earlier in the book.

Yorkshire, South Kirkby

NCB 0-6-0ST no. 6 *Fitzwilliam* is pictured in a sorry state on 6 August 1971. Built by Hunslet, works no. 1438, in 1923, the engine was ex-Hemsworth Colliery (merged with South Kirkby July 1967), arriving at South Kirkby by April 1966. Under nationalisation, *Fitzwilliam* was one of four Hunslet 0-6-0STs used at the colliery. From March 1970 'merry-go-round' coal trains worked into South Kirkby. *Fitzwilliam* survived until January 1972 when it was scrapped on site by Thos W. Ward Ltd.

Yorkshire, South Kirkby

NCB 0-6-0ST no. 9 *Kinsley* is seen in pristine condition on 6 August 1971. The engine was built by Hunslet in 1939, works no. 1954. Bradley (2002) states the loco was ex-South Elmsall, Featherstone & Hemsworth Collieries Ltd, and was inherited with the site by the NCB on 1 January 1947. *Kinsley* visited Hunslet for repairs in 1947/48 and was at New Monckton Colliery by November 1964. It arrived at South Kirkby in November 1967. In preservation, *Kinsley* moved to Steamport, Southport, in November 1975, but is currently at the Ribble Steam Railway, Preston.

Yorkshire, St John's Colliery, Normanton

St John's colliery was opened in around 1878, and there were sidings running north from the BR (ex-LMSR) Leeds Sheffield line to the colliery. Another NCB line dating from around 1950 linked St John's with Parkhill Colliery, which the latter used to reach the former's coal preparation plant. St John's closed in June 1973, followed by the CPP in March 1980. Hudswell Clarke built 0-4-0T *Cathryn* in 1955, works no. 1884. The locomotive was supplied new to Newmarket Colliery, Stanley, and after repairs in 1969, it moved to St Johns Colliery, Wakefield. *Cathryn* alternated between there and Park Hill Colliery, Wakefield, until the end of its working life in March 1977. The engine is currently with the Ecclesbourne Valley Railway.

Yorkshire, Wharncliffe Wood, nos 4-5 Colliery, Carlton

The colliery was formerly known as Carlton Main Colliery and was served by sidings on the west side of the BR (ex-LMS) line. It was also connected at the south end of the yard to a spur from the BR (ex-LNER, former Hull & Barnsley) railway line. Hunslet built 0-6-0ST, works no. 2886, in 1943 (ex-WD, Donnington Depot, Shropshire, 104). The colliery closed in July 1970. The picture was taken on 5 April 1971, six months before the loco went for scrap to Thos W. Ward Ltd of Sheffield.

Yorkshire, Wheldale Colliery

Castleford's Wheldale Colliery opened in 1868 and closed in 1987. The colliery sidings were on the north side of a BR (ex-LNER) line and situated north-east of Castleford Central railway station. Other lines linked to Fryston colliery, the south bank of the River Aire, and later Allerton Bywater colliery and spoil tips north of the river. Hunslet's 15-in. 0-6-0ST *Bawtry* was built in 1932, works no. 1698. The locomotive was ex-Airdale Collieries Ltd and spent time at Newmarket Colliery and Allerton Bywater Central Workshops before returning to Wheldale in March 1967. Under nationalisation a large proportion of Wheldale's locomotives – both steam and diesel – were from Hunslet's. Photographed in 1971, the end came for *Bawtry* in December 1972 when it was scrapped on site by W. H. Arnott, Young & Co. Ltd, Bradford.

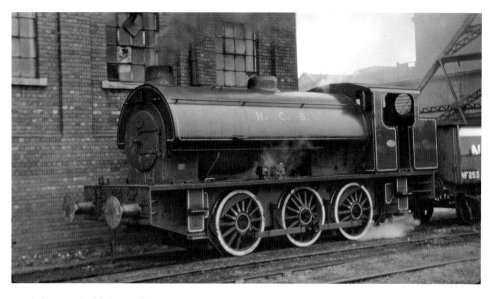

Yorkshire, Wheldale Colliery

Hunslet's 18-in. 0-6-0ST *Diana*, works no. 2879, was built in 1943, and was ex-Waterloo Main Colliery and Allerton Bywater Central Workshops before it moved to Wheldale in September 1970. The engine is seen in the fully lined NCB maroon and red livery on 16 September 1971. From Wheldale the engine migrated to Newmarket Colliery in October 1973, and from there to Springwell Central Workshops in January 1975. The engine is currently located at the Caledonian Railway (Brechin) Ltd.

Yorkshire, Woolley Colliery, Darton

The Woolley Coal Company began producing coal from drift workings in 1854. This had been encouraged by the opening of the branch railway from Wakefield to Barnsley in 1850. The colliery was situated north-east of Darton railway station. The use of surface locomotives was superseded in 1984 when a new coal preparation plant and loading bunker were erected in the area. The colliery closed in 1987. Hunslet built 0-6-0ST *Newstead*, works no.1589, in 1929. The engine spent time at South Kirkby Collieries Ltd, Hemsworth Colliery and Frickley Colliery, before arriving at Woolley in April 1966. Photographed on 6 August 1971, the engine went to M. Saul, Hertfordshire, in July 1972.